D0923394

ETHICS
DEAD
AND
ALIVE

Barrows Dunham

ETHICS
DEAD
AND
ALIVE

Alfred A. Knopf
New York 1971

THIS IS A BORZOI BOOK
PUBLISHED BY ALFRED A. KNOPF, INC.

To my granddaughter Pamela [b. 1964]

and
to the Misses Eileen Chamberlain, Edythe Clark,
Nancy Feinberg, Patricia Goldstein,
Dorothy Graham, Christine Hatch, Ann Hessler,
Lynn Kressel, Barbara Massler, Anette Seltzer,
Sheryl Treco, Ronnie Weinberg, Kathryn Wisch
—members of my class in Contemporary
Philosophy, 1968, at Beaver College,
who received me back into college teaching
after an interval of fifteen years.

. . . May God us Keep
From single vision & Newton's sleep!

WILLIAM BLAKE

CONTENTS

ETHICS
DEAD
AND
ALIVE

PART I

The
Death
of
Ethics

1
The Problem About Problems

$\mathcal{B}$EFORE WE WERE BORN, we had no problems, nor (in my view, at least) will we have them after we are dead. We have no problems, it thus seems, unless we are alive. To be alive is to have problems; but also, and somehow more pleasantly, to have problems is to be alive.

Further, to be alive is to have needs—needs (to take the least number we can) for food, clothing, shelter, play, love. If these our needs were instantly satisfied, we would still have no problems. Our state would then be as Hume described it in his elegant way: "The perpetual clemency of the seasons renders useless all clothes or covering; the raw herbage affords . . . the most delicious fare; the clear fountain, the richest beverage."[1]

In all that follows I shall be using the term "need" to signify a lack of and at the same time a striving for something without which a man either cannot live or

---

[1] *An Enquiry Concerning the Principles of Morals*, Section III, Part I, § 2. Let us complete the passage: "No laborious occupation required: no tillage, no navigation. Music, poetry, and contemplation form his sole business: conversation, mirth, and friendship his sole amusement." Hume was no doubt well acquainted with Virgil's "omnis feret omnia tellus" in the Fourth Eclogue. He was, perhaps, a little behind Virgil, who projected this upon the future, where in fact it is. For, as labor diminishes under technology, there will be the problem what to do with leisure time—time that once had been leisure. I don't know that anyone can surpass Hume's suggestions: the arts and contemplation, talk, merriment, and love.

cannot grow. He must eat, be clothed and lodged, or else he'll die; he must play, love and be loved, or else he cannot develop toward the exercise of his own powers. Care in illness and education into knowledge are necessary for both.

Now, needs give rise to wishes, the wishes being shaped and given substance by the circumstances in which the needs are immediately to be satisfied. Thus the need to eat, felt physically as hunger, gives rise to a wish for this or that specific and available food. The same thing holds, in varying ways, for all the other needs as they are felt.

It seems to be the case, morally, that the satisfaction of human needs is always and everywhere a (good) thing. To deny this would be to assert that the survival of people and their growth is morally unimportant. The limit of this tendency would be a view to the effect that neither the human race nor any of its members deserves to survive. It may be so; at any rate, we seem not to possess a definitive argument to the contrary. It is, however, a view I find incredible, and so cannot adopt.

If all human needs deserve to be satisfied—if, that is to say, it can never be intrinsically wrong to satisfy a human need—then we can say that persons, things, acts, and relations become valuable whenever they satisfy a need. It is morally important that men be fed, clothed, lodged. Hence the specific food, clothing, shelter are themselves morally important: so also the opportunities to play, to love and be loved.

Now, any act or relation or person or thing either does or does not satisfy a need at the given time. If it does so, it is morally valuable; if not, it is not valuable or perhaps defeats value. All of this is wholly "objective"; it happens regardless of anyone's opinion or possibly of anyone's observation. Accordingly, moral value is not an effect of human judgment, but is, so to say, "out there" all the time, whether it is judged to be so or not. The need is a fact, the satisfaction is a fact, and the value is a fact also. You cannot, without error, deny that it is there when it *is* there, nor, without error, assert that it is there when it is not. A great many facts, to be sure, are not values, but all values are facts.

It remains to be said that the psychological difference between needs and wishes carries with it a moral difference also. The circumstances that shape wishes and give substance to them are full of obstacles, among which may be the needs and wishes of other people. We seem disposed to cancel out obstacles by going round them or by crushing them. Hence some wishes, attempting to satisfy some needs, do so by causing harm: when this happens, other people's needs and wishes have been frustrated. From this state of affairs, which ought not to be but often *is*, derives the odious fact that on great social questions it is difficult to effect anything good without causing harm.

There is, however, a more humane and hopeful inference. Some wishes, being bad or evil, ought not to be fulfilled, while at the same time the needs they rose from do deserve to be fulfilled. This union of contraries will perhaps let us see that criminal acts, though evil in nature, had a morally valid source in sheer human need. Thus we can think that, by attending to need, we can cause the criminal wish and act to disappear. We are somewhere near to doing this, the possibility of abundance in goods and services being almost at hand. There is, however, too much anger among us; and anger, a flame that gives more smoke than light, darkens the difference between wish and need.

I I

WELL, THEN, we have needs but have not instant satisfaction. Therefore we have problems. These problems are morally of two sorts:

(1) It quite often happens within one's personal life that needs conflict with needs and wishes with wishes, because the circumstances do not allow of wider satisfaction. Thus, for example, if you elect to marry, you afterward cannot have the special delights (if such they are) of the unmarried state. If you choose one career, you will have eliminated most other careers that had been possible.

Consequently there arises the question: Which need (or wish) shall I satisfy? Any answer to this question, competent or incompetent, assumes that there is a rule by which the answer can be determined. Even acting by whim is a rule: "I'll do as I happen to like." The only alternative to deciding by a rule is to leave the event to chance. Then you would be as if you were not answering the question—as if, blindfolded, you put your hand into a bag of marbles and drew out the marble your hand happened to touch.

(2) There is, next, the conflict between one's own needs and wishes and the needs and wishes of other people. From this rises the question: Whose need or wish shall I satisfy? Any answer to this question also and equally assumes a rule. For he who decides such things to his own advantage or to the advantage of his "side" assumes a rule quite as much as a man who decides on behalf of all mankind. Indeed, the more self-interested he is and the more partisan, the more resolute he is about a rule; he would not for the life of him follow the grab bag theory of ethics. There is, he thinks, too much at stake to take chances. There is indeed.

But not all rules, though in this way unavoidably accepted and followed, are satisfactory or even rational. Suppose, for example, I were to say, "I *alone* among mankind am worth doing things for." The appropriate response would be laughter, for such a principle can convince no one—not even (if I have any sense) myself. Now, suppose I say: "I and my family and the members of my church, class, race, nation are the *only* people worth doing things for." Absurdity would still remain and even be evident, despite the covering of a thousand colors.

Apparently the case is that I can make no ultimate moral claim for myself or for the people I happen to be historically joined with that cannot also be made for people other than myself and people I happen not to be historically joined with. The only rule that can be safe from internal contradiction must embrace all mankind.

There is such a rule, often stated and very well stated too. For example, "Do unto others. . . ." But, for myself, I prefer the more rigorous Kantian version: "Treat everyone, yourself included, as an end; never treat anyone merely as a means."[2]

This rule, applied, will shape decisions and their consequences, but it will also create a proper climate of decision. It will secure that the decision is not merely self-interested, and perhaps also that the decider is not self-deceived. What it does is to make intent plain by enabling everyone else to compare it with the observable consequences. It is a form of communication. The decider shows that he asks no special privilege, no exemption from principle, and that he intends to do exactly what is

---

[2] "Handle so, dass du die Menschheit, sowohl in deiner Person, als in der Person eines jeden andern, jederzeit also Zweck, niemals bloss also Mittel brauchest." *Grundlegung zur Metaphysik der Sitten*, Zweiter Abschnitt. I suggest that this splendid title can be accurately, though less impressively, rendered as "How To Be Moral."

required of all other men. In this way he invites trust, having made himself worthy of it.

Kant's statement of the principle is not difficult, but it can be simplified. I suggest this reading: Treat everyone as worth doing things for. And the ground of the rule will be this: every human being has intrinsic worth, is morally important, just because he is a human being. A man may, of course, compromise this worth by causing intolerable harm to others. Then, I suppose, having made himself an obstacle to the general well-being, he will need at the best to be rehabilitated and at the worst to be made powerless.

I I I

ETHICAL THEORY differs from moral codes. The codes are lists of admonitions, with little or no account of why they are binding. But ethical theory undertakes to explain in some detail the procedure of right decision, of how one ought to make up one's mind. Throughout this enterprise moves an effort to escape bias. Mathematics and the other sciences assert, or try to assert, what is the case, regardless of what anyone wishes were the case. Similarly, ethical theory asserts, or tries to assert, what ought to be chosen and done, regardless of what anyone wishes were chosen and done. For, just as the darkling flow of appetite and apprehension can dim awareness of the world we act in, so also it can dim awareness of what and how to decide. To pierce the shell of the self is, in ethics or the sciences, a primary task, so that the self, emerging, may know the world and what to do about the world.

There are rules for all of this, and since they are still debated, I suppose we must regard them as tinged with doubt. But the odd fact is that there is less doubt about the rules than there is doubt about our recognizing when the rules have been successfully applied.

Take, for example, the rule that determines whether or not a sentence, an assertion, is true: "A sentence is true, if and only if what it asserts to be the case actually is the case." (Thus the sentence "Abraham Lincoln died in the year A.D. 1865" is true, because he did in fact die in that year.) The rule seems convincing (to me, entirely so), but it requires a comparison between the sentence and the objective fact. This comparison is an act that varies a great deal from ease to difficulty. Our immediate awareness is limited, possibly inaccurate, and all the extensions of awareness by telescope or microscope still retain some limitations of immediacy. Moreover, try as we may, we cannot entertain more than a relatively few instances, and from these we infer generalizations—a leap from "some" to "all." In this, as it has happened, we have been bold and successful—with, however, not a few lapses. It seems that we have knowledge without quite knowing how we got it. Accordingly, doubt dogs the scientist.

The doubt that thus dogs the scientist has less to do with the rule itself than with our efforts to apply the rule. I think that much the same thing holds in ethics. Probably there is more doubt about the rules here than in science, but, as before, it is in the applications that doubt most lies. Suppose we say that there is in ethics a rule against self-defeating behavior—part of what Kant seems to have meant by the Categorical Imperative. The rule is quite convincing, because it is plainly absurd, in working toward an end, to use means that will make the end unattainable.

Examples could always be found, of a rather narrow sort. Not until our own quite recent time have there been examples on a gigantic scale. One can now cite two violations of that rule which will involve us in a common ruin. If we continue to do, or permit to be done, what is now done, our environment will in time be uninhabitable because poisoned; and if we ever engage in nuclear warfare, the same result will occur more quickly. When that has happened, all the ends (profit, say, or power) for which those acts were done will have become unattainable, because the acts will have left no one on earth to have profit or power or anything else.

Lunacy itself cannot do so much. The ultimate catastrophe, since it takes science, takes brains. But at least absolute ruin, now a possibility, makes the rule against self-defeating actions seem cogent indeed. The other rule (also Kantian) that I have suggested for our choices—"Treat everyone as worth doing things for"—may not seem so cogent, though it is more humane and less coldly logical. Nevertheless it is certainly bound up with the prescription against absolute ruin, and an argument can be made that anti-social behavior is somehow self-defeating—at any rate, in the long run (that last resort of hopeful moralists).

Accordingly, one may think (as I do) that these two rules of ethics are very little touched with doubt. Moral doubt—the kind you have when you wonder whether you have really done right, or wonder which course of action is really the right one to follow—chiefly surrounds the applications. The main puzzle always is, how to relate principle to conduct, theory to practice; and this, as it seems, is more of an art than a science. At all events, I think it is important, in ethics or science, not to let the doubt that so much attends the applications slough over and suffuse the principles. We can still manage while doubting the applications—perhaps, indeed, we cannot manage without a little doubting the applications

(Keats's "negative capability"). But if doubt annihilates
the principles, we are lost.

We are lost, because then we have no principles to
apply to anything, and so cannot judge. There would then
be a kind of moral helplessness, a paralysis of rational
choice. No man and no act is self-justifying, self-val-
idating. Quite to the contrary, every man and every act,
in order to be justified, must be referred to principle. We
seem readily aware that this condition holds for our personal wishes. It likewise holds for statute law and social
custom. Some statutes, made in the interest of ruling
groups, are morally null and perhaps profoundly evil.
So also are some social customs. It follows that all laws
and customs are subject to review and criticism by moral
principle.

For suppose the contrary were the case. If our
wishes were self-justifying, the wish of the strongest,
prevailing, would be "right." If statute laws were self-justifying, all the discriminatory laws against Blacks would
be "right." Indeed—an interesting corollary—if laws and
customs were self-justifying, this would already be the
best of all possible worlds.

All such conclusions are, as in the wide eye of
day, brilliantly false. Moreover, most of them will show
the taint of special pleading. Mere wish or prejudice has
slid, dullingly, across the grounds of decision. From these
grounds we therefore need to fend off all special influences
of the times we live in, the people we live with, the personal characters we have. Times, people, character will
no doubt serve as *content* for theory, but they cannot
determine validity. They are not the guide of theory;
rather, theory is to guide *them*.

We may now observe, usefully, how this interplay
has happened with one of the great classical moralists,

Plato, in his concept of the ideal commonwealth. This commonwealth was to be governed by an elite, was to be an "aristocracy." Plato meant this term in its etymological sense of "government by the best." Now, Plato was a member of the then existing (though not always ruling) aristocracy, the families whose wealth lay in the ownership of land. This aristocracy, as aristocracies do, thought itself peculiarly fit to govern. There may be an inference to the effect that Plato's membership in this elite disposed him to think that government by an elite is best government.

But at just this point all such influence, if influence it was, abruptly stops. For the aristocracy of Plato's Republic was to be deprived of just those things most valued by the aristocracy he belonged to: property and family. The governing elite of the ideal commonwealth was to own no property and have no families, thus to be preserved incorruptible. Indeed, it can be argued that precisely because Plato was an aristocrat of those days, he knew the chief sources of political evil and could propose their abolition. His ideal elite was elite solely because it possessed the knowledge and the wisdom to govern. The Platonic Guardians much more resemble Marx's "vanguard of the proletariat" than they do the once living, exploitative aristocrats of ancient Athens.

It seems evident, then, that any personal bias in Plato has been profoundly modified, though not entirely removed, by the effort at impartial discussion. Exactly this effort, found among all the masters, prevents us from reducing their theories to their private tastes, their special times, the customs that then chanced to prevail. Yet the touch of time, taste, and custom was discernibly there.

I have reflected thus upon past thinkers, because,

as I wrote these pages, I grew aware that to write upon ethics is to write one's autobiography. Every pain of past decision, every puzzled ache, every smallest hesitation before an obscure consequence springs back from buried memory and demands acknowledgment.

The play of self upon material is therefore a thing for readers to regard. I owe some sort of help in this. I am aware, by struggling against them, that certain things dispose me toward certain views.

For example: human success in ethics presupposes a state of affairs such that there is nothing in our nature that will unavoidably prevent success. I dare say there can be a pessimistic ethics in the sense that one may, without contradiction, judge moral defeat to be certain and at the same time abominable. But there cannot be an ethics that is at one and the same time pessimistic and practicable, that tells us that we cannot or will not do what it also says we ought to do. There is no use advocating virtue if virtue is impossible. Christian theologians long ago drew the correct inference from moral pessimism: if men are by nature too corrupt to save themselves, they can then be saved only by some power or powers not themselves.

If, to the contrary, we suppose that men *can* save themselves, then we have to take a favorable view of mankind. We have to think that whatever in our nature is corrupt or corruptible is but obstacle and impediment, to be leaped over by that same nature itself.

I must now say that I am personally disposed to this view, for my own life among people has been happy. Moreover, during fifteen years, I have been given one, two, three, four grandchildren. Nothing more subversive of a moralist can be imagined. Grandfathers cannot be pessimists. Their immortality stretches out before them, enchantingly displayed and empirically confirmed. All the talent they lack, all the power to save, leaps in the eyes of the grandchildren.

Thus it is quite impossible for me to hold, though I can of course conceive, the notion that we human beings are helplessly and therefore hopelessly corrupt. My view of human nature is therefore favorable—as, given other circumstances, it might not have been. The view collides, no doubt, with certain observable facts. When I come, as I shall, to interpret these facts, you may look to see whether errors have issued from my love and my hope.

Again: consider my notion that ethics involves principles that are binding upon human decision. Every psychiatrist will recognize in this view a strong influence of the superego. I don't doubt that this is psychologically the case. I was born a Presbyterian, the son of a minister in that church, who moreover knew exactly what he thought. It is therefore unlikely that I would suppose ethics to be devoid of principle, dwindling to such locutions as "I like it" or "I like it and I wish you would too." I am of course aware that the emotivists, whose locutions these are, are neither scandalous nor contemptible, but I do indeed feel about them as if they were.

Nevertheless, predisposition toward a view does not make the view false. The view may have its own rational support. Passion may dispose me to think that a certain woman loves me, and at the same time it may be the case that she does so. Equally, of course, passion and predisposition will not cause a view to be true. For truth and falsity have nothing to do with passion at any time or place. Accordingly, my notion that ethics is normative and quasi-judicial is to be believed only so far as proof can support it. That will perhaps be not wonderfully far, for I know of no proof so overwhelming as to put the thing beyond dispute.

I V

THE EMOTIVISTS—philosophers who hold that ethical statements do nothing more than "evince" a feeling that somebody has at some particular time—are prominent, perhaps still dominant, in the Anglo-American tradition, of which they are, as one may say, the overripe fruit. The view remains attractive—not just because it is a cop-out from moral problems and therefore from political and social problems as well.

For suppose we grant, as I should, that proof can be offered for decisions, that appeal to principle can be made. When you do this, you find yourself passing from value to higher value, from principle to higher principle, until you come to a point where argument gives out. There you take a stand. Thus standing, you seem to be saying what the emotivists, positivists, empiricists will tell you you had been saying all along, namely: "I prefer!" In their view, your preference had steadily been determining your values, rather than the values the preferences.

But this can't really be so. Suppose a man has debauched his mother and is publicly charged with having done so. Suppose he then says to the public, in court or elsewhere: "I preferred!" Or suppose the Nazis on trial at Nuremberg had said (as significantly they did not): "We liked those crematoria, and we wish you'd like them too!" What moral suasion could there be in this? It isn't just that the acts are repellent; it is that, as everyone knows, preference itself often has no moral grounds at all. If preference were to determine morality, there would be no way to distinguish virtue from vice, or indeed good sense from lunacy.

How then can it happen that the "I prefer" is powerless in the midst of choosing, but returns nevertheless at the very edge of the grounds of choice, when argument has done all it can? I think it is because the "I prefer" has a much loftier status in ethics than has yet been supposed. Let us see how this may be.

As a matter of morals, it is quite impossible for any obligation to be binding—to be, indeed, an obligation at all—unless it has been consciously and willingly accepted. The man on whom it is to be binding must have been aware of it, have known exactly what it is, and have accepted it voluntarily, without any coercion whatever. For, in ignorance or under coercion, he does not really consent. He then has, and can have, no obligation.

This notion has a little the odor of contract law; perhaps it will be better to say that contract law has a little the aura of this notion. If the notion holds firm, as it seems it must, then none of us has a single obligation by virtue of having been born. We did not voluntarily enter life, and we knew nothing about it. Indeed, if we had known, we might have declined birth.

We did not voluntarily enter, nor did we know, any of the social organizations or ranks we were born into. If we had known, we might have declined membership. Once we are born into them, of course, the organizations and ranks start telling us what we owe them. So soon as a little hand is physically able to drop a penny into a cardboard box suitably inscribed, the long process of dues collection has begun.

But now we must let the principle and its consequences pierce us to the heart. If we can incur no obligations by having been born—an event we neither knew nor willed—how can we have incurred any obligation to be moral, to prefer the good to the bad, the right to the wrong, the sensible to the stupid? The inference must be that moral obligation, whatever it is, cannot have been entailed by birth.

If it was not entailed but nevertheless can be found existing, then it must have been accepted by an act of radically free choice. It was wholly undetermined by principle, because it was a decision to accept principle. Before that acceptance, principle can have had no regulative effect.

Thus, because we are helplessly born, we are morally free. Our personal independence and our possible rectitude were alike laid down in the very event we had nothing to do with. The basic choice—for ethics or against it—was necessarily our own, and lay beyond the reach of any other persons or powers.

This is the one and only "I prefer." Can one point to a specific time when this free decision is made? I think so. The moment comes, for anyone capable of rational decision, when, for the first time, he grows aware that other people may be important in the same way that he is important. If he decides that they are so, he freely embraces ethics. If not, he sets ethics aside, and afterward fares as he may.

V

ALL THIS is lofty enough, is comforting and ennobling, since it shows our intrinsic worth. The threat and pinch come, however, when we have to act in a world made wretched by past mistakes and wickednesses, and to do something about these. For ethics involves action, being the adaptation of right theory to right practice. It therefore lives victoriously, or dies defeated, amid the welter of contemporary events, the structure and struggles of the epoch we are in. We see things as in a certain atmosphere. The things are real enough and are what they are. We learn what they are by first seeing how they look.

In our present age, we shall be seeing principles and values in a stormy atmosphere. For there are not only the petty storms of personal competition; there are also three great sorts of social conflict, any one of which can be the death of us all. As if this were not enough, the three sorts act on one another, and there is struggle among the struggles. It may happen that human events pass out of human control.

The first sort of conflict is that among nations— for rise into nationhood, for survival as nations, for control over resources that maintain power and "prosperity." Violence of all degrees has attended these conflicts, and over them now hangs a violence definitive. Since it is as nations that men are most powerfully armed and organized for combat, conflicts among nations are the most dangerous of all.

The second sort of conflict is that between the relatively few men who make profits upon other people's labor and the very many men on whose labor profits are made. Not so long ago, this conflict appeared most plainly within the industrialized nations: capital against labor, employer against employee. When, however, there came to be empires—the British first and now the American—colonial peoples became the primary victims of exploitation, and workingmen in the imperial country were let share, though modestly, the profits. This ingenious device produced the illusion that the "class struggle" no longer existed at home. At the same time, it joined for colonial peoples the struggle against poverty with the struggle for national liberation. This is a prime example of how one sort of conflict can act upon another.

There remains now the third sort—lively but less easily defined. It is, I would say, the still active energy of an old series of revolutions that established the supremacy

of commerce over agriculture, of capitalism over feudal-
ism. The ideals of these revolutions were profoundly
anarchist, even antinomian. Liberty there was to be,
inviolable liberty. Equality there was to be, absolute
equality—that is to say, no bias in the administration of
law or in the conduct of politics. The individual person,
uncoerced, unobstructed, and unbemused, was to gain
what his talents allowed, to make of himself what he
might.

These ideals, plainly anarchist, were so because of
the ethic they were intended to defeat. Medieval society
had been hierarchical. You were what your birth made you
so far as rank in society went. You had no escape from
that rank, however narrow and destitute it might be.
But the men of commerce—producers, traders, inventors
—were in a position to discover that this notion merely
defeated human enterprise. It was an obstacle to be
removed. They removed it.

When a revolutionary class sets about demolishing
the "Establishment," it commonly speaks in the name of
all mankind. Partly it does so because the Establishment
has already been doing so, but chiefly it does so in order
to win the multitudes to its side. But when, after victory,
the promises are to be honored, they will be honored only
so far as suits the convenience of the new ruling class.
The victorious men of commerce, who later became captains of industry, could not and did not establish liberty,
equality, fraternity for all.

Of this failure our own American history gave the
most spectacular example. That all men are created equal
is asserted in our Declaration of Independence to be a
self-evident truth. Yet the man who wrote these words was
himself a slaveowner, and our Constitution, until amended
in 1868, counted a slave, for the purposes of census, as

three fifths of a person per person. How the three fifths was arrived at I do not know. But three fifths is obviously not equal to one.

If we keep to arithmetic, we can say that, according to the *ideals* of the capitalist revolution, one equals one, is neither more nor less than one. It has followed that everybody within the reach of that revolution, who, however, turned out to be treated as less than one, has striven to make good the difference. Our Blacks got only the verbal three fifths annulled in 1868. They are now demolishing the social, factual difference.

It is the same with our young people, of whatever color. They know (as how can they not?) from the coercion visited upon them that they are to kill and be killed on behalf of a late (too late) American empire. Since they are even less willing to kill than to be killed, they quickly perceive, what has long been known, that human affairs could be much better arranged.

The love of youth for life—a natural love I would suppose it to be—therefore, throughout the world, sets youth against governments, every one of which is, if not bent on slaughter, at least willing to commit it. Men against government is struggle of the anarchist sort—the sort let loose by the old capitalist revolution and not yet resolved by the socialist.

Moreover, it is the case that one country in the world, our own, is technologically equipped to produce abundance—to satisfy, that is to say, all the needs and most of the wishes of its inhabitants. The sole obstacle is the capitalist system itself, the production of goods for profit rather than for use. This system distorts production toward waste and death, these having now become the chief means of maintaining the market. Thus it may happen that the power to produce general abundance produces instead universal death.

The alternatives are staggering. Something like absolute happiness is quite possible; so also is absolute ruin. The horror we feel at absolute ruin obscures the fact that we also have a chance at absolute happiness.

The chance at happiness is a perfectly real thing in the sense that some of the necessary conditions for it do exist. These conditions also give rise to certain expectations. For example, in a society of abundance, where everyone is well cared for, one would expect also an abundance of liberties. All the competitions that scarcity promotes would have disappeared, driven out by abundance. With these would have gone repressive laws and preposterous customs, mere vestigial organs that died of nothing to do.

Given abundance of goods and services—all these supplied with ever decreasing hours of work—one would expect to be extremely free: not free from want merely— indeed, no longer free *from* anything—but free to love, to give, to grow, to make up one's own mind, untouched and untouchable by penalty or bribe.

Can it be that our young people somehow sense how near we are to abundance, and therefore ask the liberties that properly go with it? Their requests, as they state them, are mostly affirmative—not freedoms *from* but freedoms *for*: for loving, for giving, for deciding on their own. *Against* is what they are against. "Interdit d'interdire" was the slogan of the French students in May, 1968.

If this is how things are, we can understand why the young rebels come, so many of them, from prosperous families and comfortable homes. They have grown up in material plenty, and they are thus peculiarly fitted to recognize that our society does not grant the liberty which plenty should entail. Moreover, the new sexual freedom (an effect of technology) saves them from some of the deceits that used to come with adolescence. They are less

soon exposed to corruption, and thus may gather strength
to resist it.

Perhaps this is why the rebellion of youth is now
so profoundly moral—an attempt to make ethics prevail.
Theories about politics, sociology, education are at a
minimum. The youth don't give you a history of capitalist
or bureaucratic practices; they tell you, quite simply, that
the practices are wrong. Hard-bitten administrators, for
whom morality has been a cover rather than a guide, suppose this to be a cover also, and go looking (as they
suppose) underneath. What they then find is, not the
actionable conspiracies they had hoped for, but just more
morality. Cynics may well feel outraged, but they have
had this disillusionment coming to them for a long time.

The socialist revolution hoped for many gains, but
guaranteed only one. It guaranteed a set of social relations such that abundance, so soon as it became possible,
would be readily distributed for the satisfaction of every
one's needs. It guaranteed an end to poverty, and in fact
poverty does disappear wherever socialism grows. You
can see the thing for yourself by traveling from the
Soviet Union into Greece, say, or Turkey or India.

But all great struggles constrict liberty. It is true
that when the struggle is against exploitation, the exploited multitudes will feel within their gathering and
disciplined strength a freedom they had not felt before.
Yet the supreme anarchist freedoms—the ones we require
in order to be fully ourselves—need for their ground a
world-wide system of peace and plenty. The capitalist
revolution solved the problem of producing plenty. The
socialist revolution solves the problem of distributing it.
These have been great corrective events. Without them,
we would be nowhere near our happiness. Yet we are
near it—so near (as we used to say) and yet so far!

From this point of view—the broadest I am able to

take—the fierce verbal attacks, one nation upon another, one system upon another, will seem like mere chidings. The socialist powers (omitting for a time their abuse of one another) can say with entire truth that capitalism cannot distribute the abundance it produces. The capitalist powers (also omitting for a time their abuse of one another) can say with entire truth that socialism has not yet achieved the old grand anarchist ideals. To the extent that these antagonists score off one another, we are all not the wiser, but the nearer death.

There is something like lunacy in this, as of people who could not be sensible if they tried. The fact is that we can have it all—all the good, all the happiness. If we can have it all, why should we shatter it all? This question, a question of morals and sanity, I set as background for all the discourse that follows.

2

The *Is,*
the *Ought,*
and Professor Moore

---

*I*T IS MANY YEARS NOW since Professor George Edward Moore published his *Principia Ethica* (1903), the last of the classics in that form and the first alienated work of the Age of Alienation. Two remarkable events distinguish, in Western thought, those years. Ethical theory fell prostrate as if it were dead, and mankind suffered horrors inconceivable before that time, with a promise of greater horrors to come.

These two events, or series of events, did in fact happen. It is tempting to think that there may have been a causal relation between them. Can we suppose that the collapse of ethical theory freed scoundrels to torture and torture and kill and kill? Was it the case that Professor Moore, an honest, rather troubled don at Cambridge, did, by his theorizing, assist in any way the ovens at Auschwitz, the fire over Hiroshima, the fire that now burns in possibility over the entire globe?

Moore did, I think, numb the nerve of valuation, so far as theory can numb it. But in the men who decreed and wrought the horrors, the nerve of valuation was not numb but overactive, a hypertrophied part. They thought, in their bizarre and paranoid way, that they did right. Conscious rogues—men who are aware that their acts are merely selfish—seldom inflict calamities so great as those inflicted by men who imagine themselves to be acting on high moral grounds. Moreover, there are billions of folk, and have been other billions, who never knew the theory of George Edward Moore. Thus, although there are things in the theory that serve rather aptly as prologue to the horrors, the perpetrators did not know these things, and we must count Moore blameless.

The theory itself, as set forth in the *Principia* of 1903 and the *Ethics* of 1912 (a little book in the Home University Library), issued into a time of apparent calm: the Edwardian Age, which seemed to its beneficiaries the perfection of social life. For the Victorian conscience, wearied with endeavor, had grown dull; indeed, how long can calamity be pointed to and denounced without fatigue? Ruskin, the prophet, had died in 1900, his mind already gone. Swinburne, who, when young, had praised and may have enjoyed the raptures and roses of vice, was living in Putney with Watts-Dunton, the death of roses. Florence Nightingale was declining, wearied at last, into immortality.

I I

THE LAST YEARS of Victoria's reign moved through scenes of charming decadence: "l'Art pour l'Art," the drawings of Aubrey Beardsley, the facetiae of Max Beerbohm, and lesser irreverences of lesser men. The older morality, to be sure, took vengeance on Oscar Wilde, but there was a feeling that a new reign would bring new ease. The Queen died. The King lived, and waited to be crowned. And then —and then, quite suddenly on the eve of coronation, the King was stricken with appendicitis.

It takes more than argument or satire to drive old notions from the field. The King's illness, the successful

surgery, the postponed coronation, all brought forth moralizing from which "enlightened" views were notably absent.
The Bishop of Stepney, preaching at Saint Paul's, said,
"May it not be that we were all advancing to this solemn
act with undue levity and that the call has come in this
postponement to remember the Lord Our God?" And
the Bishop of Southampton, at Petersfield, said, "It might
be that we had been too much absorbed in thoughts of
Imperial greatness and earthly prosperity." Very likely it
was. And the Bishop of London, at Chapel Royal, Saint
James', said, "Every inquiring mind must ask why it happened. It is our duty to profit by experience. Were we
going to the Coronation too much as a great show, too
little as a great national sacrament?"[1]

The clergy, and no doubt many other subjects of
the King, thought the event a divine threat of punishment,
possibly even punishment delivered there and then. For
there had been sins, among them the King's own amiable
ones. He was a pleasant monarch, who liked prosperous
men and pretty women, without much regard to their
origin. It thus came to pass that Jews, if they were rich
enough, moved in the highest society, and the Wertheimer
sisters sat to Sargent. The King, moreover, would, when
he liked, visit now and then and here and there a Scots
nobleman or an Irish. And, to crown all novelty, English
peers, who had long been given to marrying actresses,
began to marry Americans.

Toward the established laws of high society, the
King, who presided over all ranks, was a subversive influence. A true *bonhomme*, a genuinely good fellow, he
liked whom he liked, as a natural man would do. People

---

[1] All these quotations will be found in William Scovill
Adams: *Edwardian Heritage* (London: Frederick Muller, Ltd.;
1949), pp. 13–14 nn. This book, I may say, is a monument to the
impressive skill of its author, now deceased.

of lesser (though still high) rank had not the privilege. The orders of society were fixed and firm, the rich conspicuously rich and the poor conspicuously poor. The beautiful Countess of Warwick, who was also a Socialist, once explained to Elinor Glyn the rules then binding upon hostesses:

> Army or naval officers, diplomats or clergymen . . . might be invited to dinner. The vicar might be invited regularly to Sunday lunch or supper, if he was a gentleman. Doctors and solicitors might be invited to garden parties, though never, of course, to lunch or dinner. Anyone engaged in the arts, the stage, trade or commerce, no matter how well connected, could not be invited to the house at all.[2]

In philosophy, the Edwardian Age presented, if not serried ranks, then at any rate serried doctrines. Doctrines existed *in corporibus* and by schools. You swallowed the whole body or you swallowed none. You could philosophize only if you had the digestion of a boa constrictor. There were the Absolute Idealists, who thought that the universe was a cosmic consciousness or even a Cosmic Person. There were the Utilitarians, who thought that all human behavior, in politics or economics or morals, was but a seeking of pleasure and an avoiding of pain. There were the Meliorists, who thought that every stage in animal evolution was a moral improvement upon its predecessor. There was Christianity, of course, in the form of a national church, a little threatened by Romanism and Nonconformity but still able to interpret the pains of the King's appendix.

There were also many ways in which life could be

---

[2] Quoted in James Laver: *Edwardian Promenade* (London: Edward Hulton; 1958), p. 21.

taken seriously. For example, instead of worrying about whom you could invite to dinner, you could have worried, and various people did worry, about providing the poor with food. In 1901, the very first year of the new reign, a book appeared under the title *Poverty*. In it the author, Seebohm Rowntree, showed that, among the poor, one newborn child in every four died within the twelvemonth.[3] The mothers, much undernourished, had little milk and were accustomed to make do with a mixture of flour and water. Public distribution of good milk came to pass in time, but, before it did so, it encountered a philosophy asserting that such distribution would perpetuate the unfit at the expense of the fit, and a theology asserting that such distribution was an interference with "God's plan."

If you survived infancy and remained poor, you might regret your survival. In 1903, Jack London published *The People of the Abyss*, a book in which he set down his extensive observation of British poverty. For example:

> There were seven rooms in this abomination called a house. In six of the rooms, twenty-odd people, of both sexes and all ages, cooked, ate, slept, and worked. In size the rooms averaged eight feet by eight feet, or possibly nine. The seventh room we entered. It was the den in which five men "sweated." It was seven feet wide by eight feet long, and the table at which the work was performed took up the major portion of the space. . . .[4]

Such was life in the Free World, when the Free World was even freer than now.

Some people have thought,[5] and some people did

---

3 Ibid., p. 176.
4 Ibid., p. 184.
5 For example, Jesus of Nazareth, in *Matthew* 25, vv. 34–40.

then think, that ethical theory has a connection with matters of this sort. It is possible to believe that the existence of poverty in the world raises the question why any people, anywhere, ought to be poor. This appears to be an ethical question, a question in philosophy, and a question of some importance.

In Edwardian times, however, Professor Moore did not touch upon this question. *Principia Ethica* was published in the same year as Jack London's *People of the Abyss,* but, though it has one paragraph about property, it has none about poverty. Since some at least of the forms of property are the reason for poverty, this may seem an oversight. But doubtless Moore's recollection (in 1941) of his procedure in earlier days is correct: "I do not think that the world or the sciences would ever have suggested to me any philosophical problems. What has suggested philosophical problems to me is things which other philosophers have said about the world or the sciences."[6]

The world, however, is difficult to avoid, though the sciences perhaps are not. While you are saying what you say, or correcting (as it may seem) what others have said, the world is doing what it does. It does more than talk, though it talks a great deal. What it does, beyond talking, is to roll and tumble. Let us take, for example, two events that bound the period within which Moore wrote.

It happened that Queen Victoria's eldest child,

---

[6] P. E. Schilpp, ed.: *The Philosophy of G. E. Moore* (Evanston, Ill.: Library of Living Philosophers; 1942), p. 14. One day in 1915, Lytton Strachey, worried by carnage at the battlefront, had a conversation with Moore, his old teacher. Strachey reports the conversation thus, in a letter to Francis Birrell (August, 1915): "When I last saw him [Moore] I asked him whether the war had made any difference to him. He paused for thought, and then said—'None. Why should it?' I asked whether he wasn't horrified by it—at any rate at the beginning. But no: he had never felt anything about it at all." Michael Holroyd: *Lytton Strachey* (New York: Holt, Rinehart and Winston; 1968), II, p. 148.

also named Victoria, married the heir to the Prussian throne. He and his princess became parents of a son Wilhelm, the Kaiser Bill of my youthful memories. About the year 1879, before she was yet Empress, Viktoria (we will give her the German spelling) read a famous book of the nineteenth century, *Das Kapital*. She sent an Englishman to call upon the author, Karl Marx. His report is one of the wonders of human prophecy. For the report was that Marx was not the man "who will turn the world upside down."[7]

Forty years later, on November 1, 1918, the son Wilhelm, being advised to abdicate, replied, "I have no intention of quitting the throne because of a few hundred Jews and a thousand workmen."[8] The ideas of the man who would not turn the world upside down had overturned two governments in Russia and were momentarily carrying workers toward power (though they did not reach it) along the streets of Berlin. Wilhelm himself was at headquarters near the collapsing front in northern France. A week later, he slipped away, no longer an emperor, into Holland.

That the glories of this world pass swiftly is a familiar fact. In high politics, competitors play (as they like to put it) "for keeps." Yet in this they are deluded, for, although everything is played for, nothing is kept. There are inferences to be drawn concerning the moral life: the certainties of peace, for example, as against the uncertainties of war. But if to any philosopher the world suggests no problems, why, then, that philosopher has a very big problem with the world.

---

[7] Michael Balfour: *The Kaiser and His Times* (Cambridge: Houghton, Mifflin Co.; 1964), p. 64 and *n*.
[8] Ibid., p. 402.

I I I

THE YEAR 1903, however, was a time when a philosopher
might think he had no problem with the world. It is difficult now to conceive such a time. Bertrand Russell remarked in a filmed interview on his eightieth birthday
that no one who did not know the European world as it
was before 1914 could know the immensity of the change.
The fact is so indeed, and Russell was the man to report
it. He was born in 1872. The godfather (*in absentia*) at
his christening in Westminster Abbey was John Stuart
Mill, who, it is said, had to overcome certain anti-religious
scruples before accepting the office. His grandfather was
Lord John Russell, the eminent prime minister; and I
have heard the grandson let fall in a lecture the words,
"As my grandfather said to Queen Victoria. . . ."

In the early 1890s, Russell was at Cambridge,
where he met George Edward Moore, two years his junior
in academic status. Moore's account is that Russell "must
have formed the opinion, from hearing me argue with
himself or with friends of ours, that I had some aptitude
for philosophy."[9]

The account is perhaps unduly modest: Moore had
aptitude for philosophy. He also had a gift for making
other men lose confidence in their ability to philosophize.
The device was to find other people's remarks hopelessly
obscure: "I *simply* don't understand *what* he means."[10]
And then, "if told something particularly astonishing or

---

[9] Schilpp: *G. E. Moore*, p. 13. Holroyd says, (in *Lytton
Strachey*, I, p. 128) that Russell once asked: "You don't like me,
do you, Moore?"—to which Moore, after characteristically careful
reflection, answered: "No."

[10] Quoted by Leonard Woolf: *Sowing* (New York: Harcourt,
Brace & Co.; 1960), p. 149. The italics are Woolf's, to show, of
course, Moore's spoken emphasis. The next quotation is from p. 151.

confronted by some absurd statement at the crisis of an argument, his eyes would open wide, his eyebrows shoot up, and his tongue shoot out of his mouth."

He could do all this in written or printed prose also. For example, in a letter to Woolf, he remarked about his own brother, the poet T. Sturge Moore:

> My brother has just published a book on Dürer. There is a great deal of philosophy in it, which begins with this sentence: "I conceive the human reason to be the antagonist of all forces other than itself." I do wish people wouldn't write such silly things—things, which, one would have thought, it is so perfectly easy to see to be just false.[11]

If you happened not to be the object of those shooting eyebrows and that shooting tongue, if, to the contrary, you could watch someone else wither beneath allegations of unclarity, you might have enjoyed the spectacle. Such is the joy we take in others' sorrows. Among Moore's students were some who escaped more often than not, who were brilliant in their own right, and who in time became famous. Besides Woolf, there were Lytton Strachey, the sour-sweet biographer; Keynes, the "savior" of capitalism; Forster, the poignant novelist; Desmond MacCarthy, David Garnett, Clive Bell. Woolf and Bell married the two Stephen sisters, Virginia and Vanessa. Out of all these people grew the Bloomsbury Group, once celebrated, which has, I suppose, left the world wiser for having been.

Moore's influence, Keynes later wrote, "was not only

---

[11] Ibid., p. 153. It may be observed that Sturge Moore's assertion, though not clear, is also not obviously false. If it means that thinking is different from anything else men do, and that it is in some sort of contest with those other activities, then the assertion is perfectly plain and perfectly true.

overwhelming; but it was the extreme opposite of what Strachey used to call *funeste;* it was exciting, exhilarating, the beginning of a renaissance, the opening of a new heaven on a new earth, we were the forerunners of a new dispensation, we were not afraid of anything."[12] Older philosophies, more stately, more admired, had been things to be afraid of, but Moore had made groundless all such fears. Other things there were to be feared, no doubt: the stirrings of the proletariat, the bellicosity of nations. But Moore had taught his disciples not to take their philosophical problems from the world or the sciences but only from other philosophers. Thus, while seeming radical and new, they shared the twilight glow of Edwardian stability. At the same time, the dissolution they introduced into things long thought exactly matched the inward social dissolution of things long done. There were to be, though they did not know it, horrors manifold; and Moore, though he did not know it, had numbed the nerve of valuation.

Indeed, quite the opposite seemed to have happened. The disciples, far from being depressed, felt themselves to be inhabiting an exalted world:

> The New Testament [wrote Keynes] is a handbook for politicians compared with the unworldliness of Moore's chapter on "The Ideal." I know no equal to it in literature since Plato. And it is better than Plato because it is quite free from *fancy.* It conveys the beauty of the literalness of Moore's mind, the pure and passionate intensity of his vision, *un*fanciful and *un*dressed-up. Moore had a nightmare once in which he could not distinguish propositions from tables. But even when he was awake, he could not

---

[12] John Maynard Keynes: *Two Memoirs* (London: Rupert Hart-Davis; 1949), p. 82.

distinguish love and beauty and truth from the furniture. They took on the same definition of outline, the same stable, solid, objective qualities and common-sense reality.[13]

That nightmare, an anxiety dream, expressed a fear of confounding words with things—of taking problems, not from the world, but from other philosophers. This, by his own assertion, is what Moore did; it is, moreover, what a great deal of Western philosophy has done after him. Since dreams are candid self-revelation, it will appear that Moore's unconscious mind possessed all the evidence necessary to refute his conscious doctrines.

The eyebrows and the tongue, shooting as they did in speech or print, have terrified—perhaps, indeed, terrorized—moralists. The doom they thus pronounced, which sounded not very loudly in 1903, lay in Moore's detection of an error (if it is an error), widespread and fatal (or so he thought), which with great verbal skill he called the "naturalistic fallacy." Let us try, now, to say what this fallacy is.

I V

I SAY "try to say" because I'm not at all sure that I can. I have followed Moore's various arguments each to a certain distance, but there always comes the moment when I can see no farther, though something appears to be there: now fades the glimmering landscape on the sight. And then I *simply* don't understand *what* he means. Analysis will produce this effect quite as much as lack of analysis. The difference is that, with lack of analysis, the fault

---

[13] Ibid., p. 94. Italics Keynes's. "The Ideal" is Chapter VI of *Principia Ethica*.

seems to be the writer's, whereas, with analysis, the fault seems to be the reader's.

Well, I'll try, anyway (though, to tell the truth, this kind of discussion is tiresome in the extreme). The basic assertion in *Principia* is that our adjective "good" refers to a *quality.* This quality can appear on an indefinite number of occasions: in acts, states, persons, things. It is, moreover, *simple,* in the sense that it has no parts. Some qualities do have parts: the quality "equine," for example, because a horse is an organization of parts. Thus if anything is to be like a horse ("equine"), it will have to have parts and thus will have the quality of having parts. But the quality called "good," so Moore thought, has no parts and is, accordingly, simple.

A second assumption in *Principia* is that a definition, in order to be *logically* compelling, has to describe a system of organized parts. Dictionary definitions are not, or are not necessarily, of this logically compelling sort, for, a good part of the time, they tell you not what the thing is but how the word is used by people who speak the language at the given time. You can get a definition of "equine" that will state what the quality really is, regardless of vagaries of usage.[14] But there is not (or seems not to be) any such definition for the adjective "good." Accordingly, so Moore wrote, "the peculiar predicate [i.e. "good"], by reference to which the sphere of Ethics must be defined, is simple, unanalyzable, indefinable."[15]

This result is staggering, for it leaves us quite unable to say what the most important term in ethical discourse means. Disputes in ethics seem in the end to be quarrels about how the term is to be defined. If it can't be

---

14 *Principia,* § 8.
15 Ibid., § 24.

defined at all, the disputes are senseless, a notion that has been lively in the years since *Principia.*

The result is also staggering as regards the work of the great moralists. I suppose few men have read Plato's account of harmony in the self and in society, as the *Republic* gives it, without feeling they knew more about the moral life than they had previously known. The same also with Spinoza's account of human freedom in *Ethics,* Part V, and with Kant's austere celebration of moral law in the *Grundlegung.* But if the adjective "good" is in fact indefinable, all these grand attempts were vain. Moore himself rejected them, and found indeed only one moralist other than himself aware of the naturalistic fallacy: Professor Henry Sidgwick.[16]

For the "fallacy," as we can now perhaps see, lies in trying to define the indefinable adjective "good," in saying that "good" means "such-and-such." This will happen, for example, if you say, "good" means "pleasant," or "good" means "self-disciplined," or "good" means "conscientious." Moore is quite willing for you to say, "Conscientiousness is good," "Self-discipline is good," "Pleasure is good." But in these assertions the predicate "good" is always something other than, and added to, the subject. That is to say, the quality "good" will perhaps be found in conscientiousness or self-discipline or pleasure, but, being always distinguishable from them, cannot be identified with them.

But perhaps we shall more readily discover why Moore thought "good" to be indefinable if we consider his celebrated analogy between "good" and "yellow." "Just as you cannot," wrote Moore, "by any manner of means, explain to anyone who does not already know it, what yellow is, so you cannot explain what good is."[17] Now,

---

16 Ibid., § 14.
17 Ibid., § 7.

"yellow" can of course be defined in terms of what Moore calls its "physical equivalent."[18] But that is not (or is it?) the *seen* yellow. Conceivably the *seen* yellow could also be physiologically defined; and if you are a philosophical materialist, you may be content to stop there. But Moore was not a philosophical materialist. He was an empiricist in the true British style. He thought that you had (or, possibly, were) a consciousness, in which sense-qualities directly present themselves, and other qualities too in much the same manner. Your knowledge of the qualities comes from your direct awareness of them and only from *your* awareness. Nobody else can tell you. The knowledge is intuitive.

Thus a man knows what "yellow" means, by having seen the color with a normal human eye. He knows what "good" means, by having intuited the quality in various acts, states, persons (are we to add, with a normal moral sensitivity?). A blind man can't see yellow. Are we to suppose that a man who can't intuit the quality "good" has some comparable defect? Yet moral intuition (if there is such a thing) is obviously not sensory intuition, and a great many more people will agree about "yellow" than will agree about "good."

Moore seems not to have any very exact account of moral intuition, and tends to treat it in the style of Hume and Adam Smith, as a matter of the moral sentiments. He undoubtedly thought that the quality "good" *can* be intuited, and that it is normative in the sense that it causes some choices to be preferable, even decidedly preferable, to others. Some things, indeed, he believed to be intrinsically good or intrinsically bad—that is, good or

---

[18] E.g., the definition of "yellow" in Webster's Collegiate of 1936: "That one of the four psychological primaries which is seen when energy of wave length 574.5 mμ is employed as a stimulus."

bad whenever and wherever they appear. We shall discuss these later and with some astonishment.

I have said that Moore numbed the nerve of valuation. What did the numbing was the doctrine that "good"
is indefinable. For this doctrine deprives us of any means
of making our notion of "good" public. I might point to a
person and say: "In him I intuit the quality 'good.'" But
you, if you looked at that person, would find and say—
what? Suppose you said, "Yes, I too intuit the quality
'good' in him"—how would you know that you and I,
though using the same word, mean the same quality? Or
again: some men, looking at the furnaces at Auschwitz,
would intuit the quality "bad." It is notorious, however,
that some thousands of Nazis looked at those same furnaces and intuited the quality "good." Presumably these
two intuitions cannot both be correct. But if the adjective
"good" is indefinable, how can we know which of them is
correct and which not? Or how can we know even whether
the two intuitions are contradictory?

Throughout his argument, Moore proceeds as if he
were laying bare what is self-evidently the case, and he
does this so skillfully that many philosophers after him
have thought that this really was self-evidently the case.
For example, no proof is given for the two fundamental
assertions, that the quality "good" is simple and that simple qualities cannot be defined. These assertions are taken
to be self-evident. But probably there are no self-evident
assertions at all; or, if there are, these two are not obviously among them. Bernard Bosanquet, a leading philosopher when Moore was just a rising one, reviewing
Principia on its appearance,[19] wrote that any term what-

---

[19] In the journal *Mind*, 1903. Professor Alasdair MacIntyre
remarks, with deadly accuracy, "More unwarranted and unwar-
rantable assertions are perhaps made in *Principia Ethica* than in
any other single book of moral philosophy, but they are made with

ever can be defined. And indeed why not? All that is required is a second locution which refers precisely to the
same thing that the term to be defined referred to.

And why should we suppose that the quality "good"
is simple? The moral life is itself a complicated affair of
many parts: it involves our personal needs and wishes
and our relations with our fellow men. I would think
Plato's account of personal and social harmony more ade-
quate to the subject than the notion of a floating quality,
caught here and there by intuition, can possibly be. I
think it not unreasonable to believe that "good," if it is a
quality, is at any rate not simple—or even that it may
not be a mere quality, after all.

V

THE NATURALISTIC FALLACY is an attempt to define the
indefinable. But Moore's powerful attack on hedonism, in
the third chapter of *Principia,* has made one species of
the fallacy memorable—so memorable, indeed, that it is
what you first think of whenever the phrase is used. Any
attempt to convert fact directly into value, an *is* into an
ought, commits the naturalistic fallacy, and does so
vividly.

The Earl Russell's godfather, John Stuart Mill, was
a more than usually candid man. He wrote exactly what
he thought at the time of writing. He had the courage for
this—and it takes courage. For, at any time of writing,
the thought written may well be more than argument permits: it is, however, one's best insight at that particular
moment. After this manner, in the third paragraph of

---

such well-mannered, although slightly browbeating certitude, that
it seems almost gross to disagree." *A Short History of Ethics* (London: Routledge and Kegan Paul; 1967), p. 250.

Chapter IV of *Utilitarianism*, John Stuart Mill wrote the following: "The only proof capable of being given that an object is visible, is that people actually see it. The only proof that a sound is audible, is that people hear it; and so of the other sources of our experience. In like manner, I apprehend, the sole evidence it is possible to produce that anything is desirable, is that people do actually desire it."

Alas for that "in like manner"! The manner is, in fact, exactly unlike. "Visible" no doubt means "able to be seen," and "audible" means "able to be heard"; but "desirable" means "worthy to be desired," and never means "able to be desired" or "is desired." Equally, "visible" never means "worthy to be seen," and "audible" never means "worthy to be heard," though we might get such meanings out of "seeable" and "listenable."

Mill was misled by similarity of suffixes, and the true moral perhaps is that philosophers ought not to play around with mere words. From this blunder, most charmingly evident and indeed gracious (since it shows that amateurs can hardly do worse), Moore drew the inference, which everybody (including Mill) has known well enough, that you can't decide what ought to be, upon the mere evidence of what people actually want. For if what ought to be were identical with what is desired, there would not be a *moral* problem in the whole wide world, but only a problem of making one's wishes prevail. There would be, that is to say, problems of power but none of ethics.

"Hypocrisy," La Rochefoucauld remarked in a famous epigram, "is the homage that vice pays to virtue." Propaganda, we may similarly say, is the homage that power pays to ethics. What happens in politics is the effort of rulers to make their wishes prevail, but rulers generally understand that they cannot do this without presenting the wishes as morally valid—as "good," or "right," or

"just." Nothing of this sort would be necessary if the
governed were so innocent as to confuse the desired with
the desirable. As a simple matter of government, therefore, it is assumed that everybody understands the naturalistic fallacy.

We deal here, indeed, with what is perhaps the
most familiar fact of the moral life—a fact each of us has
known from a time very near to infancy. The entire contest between appetite and conscience, between (if one
cares to be Freudian) id and superego, is the struggle between what we would like to do and what we think we
ought to do: "The law in my members warring against
the law of my mind," as Saint Paul said.[20] Or, as Plato
has it in a celebrated image, the soul is like a charioteer
who drives two horses, one disciplined, one unruly.[21]
Members against mind, indiscipline against discipline—
who has not known and painfully felt the naturalistic fallacy? So subtle is life, so piercing the world, that Professor
Moore, who thought to take his philosophical problems
from other philosophers, took this one at any rate from
the world and from life in the world.

V I

THE SUPPOSED INDEFINABILITY of "good" and the risks of
the naturalistic fallacy leave us in much doubt as to what
can be done in theoretical ethics. By an odd chance, it is
perhaps the case that Moore himself had fewer doubts
than we who follow him. For there are some things that
Moore is very sure of: he is sure that there is a quality answerable to the adjective "good," and he is no less sure of
his own ability to intuit it. I will wager that few moralists

---

[20] Romans 7: 23.
[21] *Phaedrus*, 246 a–b.

would now venture to make up a list of intrinsic goods and evils (goods, that is to say, that are never other than good; evils that are never other than evil). But Moore had no hesitancy at all.

The intrinsically good things, Moore says, are "certain states of consciousness, which may be roughly described as the pleasures of human intercourse and the enjoyment of beautiful objects."[22] The phrase "pleasures of human intercourse" is fairly vague, but presumably it signifies the delights of friendship or of simple sociability. As we shall see, it decidedly does not refer to sexual intercourse.

The intrinsically evil things are cruelty, lasciviousness, hatred, envy, contempt, and pain.[23]

I suppose that not many of us would want to deny that the goods thus named are truly good and the evils truly evil. Yet, unless our intuition works precisely like Moore's, we may find ourselves short of other agreement. It turns out, for example, that Moore's notion of "lasciviousness" (or "lust," a synonym) covers all pleasure in sexual intercourse, however approved and licit the form:

> With regard to the pleasures of lust, the nature of the cognition, by the presence of which they are to be defined, is somewhat difficult to analyze. But it appears to include both cognitions of organic sensations and perceptions of states of the body, of which the enjoyment is certainly an evil in itself. So far as these are concerned, lasciviousness would, then, include in its essence an admiring contemplation of what is ugly. But certainly one of its commonest

---

[22] *Principia*, § 113. Moore was a good pianist and singer, who could charmingly perform Beethoven sonatas or Schubert *lieder*.

[23] Ibid., §§ 125–7.

ingredients, in its worst forms, is an enjoyment of the same state of mind in other people: and in this case it would therefore also include a love of what is evil.[24]

In a passage like this you will perhaps find Moore's clarity something less than clear: it has been clouded by the same timidity that once made people call table legs "limbs." Such phrases as "cognitions of organic sensations" and "perceptions of states of the body" would be accurate enough, but the things they refer to (the male lying happily with the female) make them altogether ludicrous.

Further, you may have previously supposed that lasciviousness, or lust, had to do with excess or compul-

---

[24] Ibid., § 125. This extraordinary doctrine had been a favorite of Moore's for many years. Edward Marsh, writing to Russell on November 21, 1894, said: "Have you heard about Moore's paper on Friendship? There's not much to say about it, as it was a specification of one's own ideal more or less, without much practical bearing. Of course our poor old friend copulation came in for its usual slating. . . ." (*The Autobiography of Bertrand Russell* [Boston: Little, Brown & Co.; 1967], I, p. 172). Presumably it was to this same paper that Russell referred in a letter to his fiancée, Alys, December 9, 1894: "Moore read about lust and set forth exactly thy [Alys was a Quaker] former ideal. . . . His paper did not give any good arguments, but was beautifully written in many parts, and made me very fond of him. A year ago I should have agreed with every word—as it was, I spoke perfectly frankly and said there need be nothing lustful in copulation where a spiritual love was the predominant thing, but the spiritual love might seek it as the highest expression of union. Everybody else agreed with me, except McT. [McTaggart] who came in after the discussion was over. Crompton was very good indeed and quite worsted Moore, though Moore would not admit it" (Ibid., p. 156). Moore's paper was read before the Apostles, an informal but very old club of intellectuals at Cambridge (Tennyson was once a member). Of this group Holroyd writes: "From going through the Society's papers in his role as secretary, Lytton [Strachey] had become convinced that many past Apostles were in fact secret and non-practising homosexuals. But in those unenlightened times some of them had not even been fully aware of their predilections. . . . Now, in the new uninhibited age of reason heralded by Moore, all this was to be altered." (*Lytton Strachey*, I, 208)

siveness of appetite. But if you will reread the passage often enough to make Moore's clarity clear, you will find him saying that sexual desire is an evil in itself and that it is still more evil when it evokes and enjoys a response. If you, a man, desire a certain woman, and if she desires you, and if each of you enjoys the other's desire (not to mention fulfillment), why, that is one of the worst of evils, according to George Edward Moore.

Such notions are said to be Victorian, though I will wager the Queen herself knew better.[25] They were also Edwardian, despite the King's well-known susceptibility. "I remember, in this regard," says Sir Lawrence Jones, "a small dinner-party with 'A. P.', an Oxford doctor who coached the Magdalene boat. . . . It was a party of under-graduates, and over the port one of our number boldly asked 'A. P.' whether women enjoyed sexual intercourse. 'Speaking as a doctor,' said 'A. P.', 'I can tell you that nine out of ten women are indifferent to or actively dislike it; the tenth, who enjoys it, is a harlot.' We accepted this, from such an authority, as gospel."[26]

Intuition, it will appear, is much influenced, though not always decisively influenced, by the past and present of the society one lives in. I would think that it can be

---

[25] The London Times Literary Supplement for January 2, 1969, has a review (p. 13) of *Dearest Mama*, a collection of letters between Queen Victoria and the Crown Princess of Prussia, 1861–1864, edited by Roger Fulford. The reviewer writes, quoting from the letters: "But most of all the Queen missed the personal companionship with her husband: she grieved for him so much because she had loved him so dearly. 'How much I was in love with him!' she exclaims with touching candor. And although she wrote with distaste of 'the peculiar nature of the intimacies between husband and wife,' there is no doubt that she missed those intimacies; she recalls despairingly how she had lain 'in those blessed arms clasped and held tight in the sacred hours at night, when the world seemed only to be ourselves.' "

[26] *An Edwardian Youth* (London: Macmillan & Co.; 1956), pp. 162–3.

trusted, if at all, only as the very last act in a large argument that has been leading toward ultimates. Short of this, or unconnected with rational argument, intuition is worth nearly nothing. The Nazis robbed it of its last dignity when they recommended "thinking with the blood." They did not confer many blessings, but this was one of the few.

V I I

MOORE LIVED into the atomic age, and so was aware that there existed a means of destroying the whole human race. He could also have gathered, and perhaps did gather, from the speeches of statesmen, that there might be occasions when these means would be used, with their consequent effects. I do not know what, in the light of these facts, he thought about a passage he had put in *Principia* (§ 95) some fifty years before:

> In order to prove that murder, if it were so universally adopted as to cause the speedy extermination of the race, would not be good as a means, we should have to disprove the main contention of pessimism —namely, that the existence of human life is on the whole an evil. And the view of pessimism, however strongly we can be convinced of its truth or falsehood, is one which never has been either proved or refuted conclusively. That universal murder would not be a good thing at this moment can therefore not be proved.

The last sentence has a squinting modifier, "at this moment." But no matter. For, whether Moore means "a good thing at this moment" or "at this moment cannot be proved," I think we will know what to make of a moralist who can so calmly and equably view the possible extermination of mankind. What would become of all those "intrinsic values"—"the pleasures of human intercourse and the enjoyment of beautiful objects"—in a death so universal? Beethoven and Schubert, immortal as things now stand, would lose their immortality; there would not be a finger left to play with nor an ear to hear with. All the mighty works of men would, along with their sins and errors, be consumed.

To a man in the bloody, writhing depths of the twentieth century it may seem strange that a corpus of such doctrines was ever thought liberating. Two reasons will perhaps explain why. Moore's young disciples were happy to be rid, or to seem to be rid, of their formidable elders (Mill, Kant, Spinoza); and, secondly, ethics wears a different aspect when you are in ease, from the aspect it wears when you are in trouble. When you are in ease, all problems are theoretical, except the problem of keeping yourself in ease. You then entertain schematic but fanciful possibilities: if twenty men are adrift and starving, ought they to kill and eat the fattest among them? In short, when you are in ease, ethical theory becomes casuistry. One is therefore not surprised to be told in *Principia* (§ 4) that "casuistry is the goal of ethical investigation."

But I think, for my own part, that casuistry, so far from being the "goal" of ethics, is its fatal limit, the point at which ethics ceases to be. For, although it purports to be the method of applying general rules to particular cases, it commonly shows more interest in the particularity of the cases than in the integrity of the rules. On the whole, in the moral life, as calculation advances, ethics retreats. We are left with an untidy scene, in which individual persons scramble to relax the application of rules, or ponder strange problems they will never have to face.

No doubt Professor Moore, observing the possible

extinction of mankind, was able to intuit the quality "bad" in such an event; or, intuition failing, he could have inferred the badness from his belief that cruelty is intrinsically evil. Or, failing both of these, he could have accepted the doctrine from Russell, who had always thought that our race ought to survive.

Russell, as we know, did a great deal to prevent catastrophe during the Cuban crisis of 1962. And, before that, there had been a gallant moment when Russell sat, almost ninety years old, in the rain on a platform in Trafalgar Square, to denounce the hydrogen bomb and all its uses. It is difficult to imagine Moore's sharing that platform and that rain. A failure of intuition perhaps, a fear of the naturalistic fallacy. And of course it is the case that pessimism has not yet been disproved.

3

Is It Good
If I Like It?

WE SAID at the end of Chapter 1 that the inhabitants of earth now can have it all or lose it all. There can be general abundance or general ruin. These are alternatives and therefore an occasion for choosing. To all such occasions ethics is of course relevant. Indeed, if ethics were not relevant to this the most important of all occasions, ethics would have to acknowledge itself sterile and retire.

The powers possessing nuclear weapons have spent in the last twenty years, it has been estimated, more than one *trillion* dollars on such armament. Many millions or billions have also been spent on gases and germs. If we are to predict the future behavior of nations by the devices they spend money for, the outlook is gloomy indeed. And this inference, merely factual, is dogged by a moral estimate, namely, that so foolish an animal species deserves what it gets.

Accordingly, we, as we now live and act and fear, have been put—not in mere theory, but in theory related to practice—the ultimate question. Ought we to—is there any reason why we should—would it be a good thing if we did—is it desirable that we do—survive as a species, a race, an assemblage of persons? If ethics cannot answer Yes, then it consents to its own extinction: it finds and supplies no reason why we (not perhaps very lovable), our children (very lovable), our grandchildren (adorable, with promise of yet more adorable generations to come) ought to survive.

It seems absurdly feeble to point out that ethics, if it said this, would defeat itself. One would not have thought it necessary to interpose a bare logical self-contradiction between the life of all and the death of all. The logic is there, all right, stalwart and formidable. Why not also the wish, the passion, the sense of ought? And why did Professor Moore contemplate so calmly the annihilation of mankind, on the thin ground that pessimism had not been disproved?

Moore, of course, had not the possibility before him. He was like a candidate not yet in office, who can discuss calamities which, in office, he would avoid. But even in imagination, one might think, the death of our race would put a man past contemplation of the theoretical merits of pessimism. He who does not readily perceive that mankind ought to survive is no moralist. He has already abandoned the grounds on which there can be morality, namely, that there be people. His written theory will perish with him in the holocaust. And perhaps some newborn angel, prying among the cinders, deciphering with splendid scholarship the odious script, will laugh to find a moralist who did not know whether morality ought to be.

Moore's successors would be found in worse plight, though equally incinerated—the last equality, perhaps, of men. For some at least of those successors have said that the words in our ethical vocabulary—"good," "bad," "right," "wrong"—have no more signification than sighs of approval or grunts of disapproval, ogles of entreaty or frowns of deterrence.[1] Mill himself, though (as we know)

---

[1] For the sighs-and-grunts theory, see A. J. Ayer: *Language, Truth and Logic* (New York: Oxford University Press; 1936), p. 158: "If I say to someone, 'You acted wrongly in stealing that money,' I am not stating anything more than if I had simply said,

fallible, had believed that "it is better to be a human being dissatisfied than a pig satisfied."[2] But the philosophical empiricists of our century have reduced the human being to the pig, who grunts likes and dislikes, persuasion and dissuasion, impressive toward his kind. For this, and this only, can be the meaning of the verb "evince." You would be sighing: "Gee, I like it!" You would be grunting: "Ugh, I don't like it!" You would be glancing a plea: "Gosh, I wish you would!" You would be frowning: "Damn, I wish you wouldn't!" And that would be all. There would be no notion of a rule governing your behavior and everyone else's; no notion of an end to be preferred, worthy to be desired, obligatory to be sought.

The philosophers who said these things came in time to be called "emotivists," because they held that moral judgments express how you feel about a certain thing and how you want other people to feel about it. The feelings of these emotivists happened to be remarkably tame. But we shall shortly see how certain staunch and practicing emotivists felt, and what they did.

Meanwhile, from 1914 onward, ethical theory in

'You stole that money.' In adding that this action is wrong I am not making any further statement about it. I am simply evincing my moral disapproval of it. It is as if I had said, 'You stole that money,' in a peculiar tone of horror, or written it with the addition of some special exclamation marks."

For the ogles-and-frowns theory, see C. L. Stevenson: *Facts and Values* (New Haven: Yale University Press; 1963), p. 16: "Another example: A munitions maker declares that war is a good thing. If he merely approved of it, he would not have to insist so strongly nor grow so excited in his argument. . . . If he merely meant that most people would approve of it if they knew the consequences, he would have to yield his point if it were proved that this was not so. But he would not do this, nor does consistency require it. He is not *describing* the state of people's approval; he is trying to change it by his influence." Italics Stevenson's. The essay in which this passage appears belongs to the year 1937. This date and the date of Ayer's book (1936) are important to keep in mind.

2 *Utilitarianism*, Chapter II.

the West, pinned like a butterfly upon its board by fear of the naturalistic fallacy, encountered, quite passively, a series of events.

I I

IT WILL BE REMEMBERED, from the last chapter, that the Emperor Wilhelm II, who had refused to abdicate "because of a few hundred Jews and a thousand workmen," did indeed abdicate on November 8, 1918. Two days later, news of this event reached a military hospital northeast of Berlin. One patient fell back upon his cot and wept. "So it had all been in vain," he cried within himself, "in vain all the sacrifices and privations. . . . Did all this happen only so that a gang of wretched criminals could lay hands on the Fatherland?"[3] These tears of rage were wept by Adolf Hitler, and they became in time a baleful storm.

The Edwardian Age had vanished in blood. It survived the King by a little, but it could not survive its own misconceptions. Partly, it had thought mankind too sensible and civilized for war; partly, it had thought that war, if war did occur, would be brief and glorious. Was not power balanced throughout Europe with an exquisite nicety? Were not kings, emperors, tsars, even presidents, in their proper, consecrated relations to God?

A nice balance is an equal balance, and if the sides contend, they contend equally. The European statesmen of that age had calculated to perfection. The balance of opposed power was so nearly equal that when it passed from peace into war, thirty million people died (in com-

---

[3] Quoted from *Mein Kampf* by William L. Shirer, who translates the passage, in *The Rise and Fall of the Third Reich*, paperback edition (Greenwich: Fawcett Publications; 1962), p. 52.

bat, plague, or famine) without a victory. And God himself was so far caught in reciprocal obligations that He
could make no peace.

There was, to be sure, what was called "a cessation
of hostilities." Frenchmen, Englishmen, and Americans
killed Germans and were killed by Germans until eleven
o'clock on the morning of November 11, 1918. Then they
set these matters aside for another twenty-one years.
There was a truce among them—a truce of exhaustion,
but also suddenly of a common interest among their
rulers. For, looming not far to the East, there appeared
what those rulers, well acquainted with eschatology, took
to be Satan in visible form: the world's first socialist republic. The specter that Marx had described as haunting
Europe now haunted the world.

Men show forth their dignities in their dress. Those
had been the days of plumes waving from helmets, of the
skull and crossbones adorning the Death Hussars (how
can you be important if you don't kill?), of the long morn-
ingcoat with satin lapels, of the high hat, of crowns and
tiaras—as if every elevation upon the human head
brought one nearer heaven. I remember from my boyhood
pictures of the Kronprinz Wilhelm, the Kaiser's son,
swamped beneath that furred hat with the skull and crossbones—a sad, not ungenial wretch, who had no great
taste for killing, and much preferred the love of women.

Class jostled class in those days, as now, but over
and beyond these jostlings stood the nations. Nations
have a long history, but nationhood has not. It is a gift,
a concomitant at least, of the victory of commerce over
agriculture during the past five hundred years. A nation—
any nation—can be defined by possession of a common
territory, a common government, a common system of
production, a common market, a common tradition, and

usually but not always a common language. Most of all, however, a nation can be defined as possessing a common apparatus of armed defense or armed attack. Despite the internationalism that socialists have long professed, nowhere is any class armed against any other class in the way that nations are armed against nations, unless the class has happened to seize national power.

Therefore, so far as power and its present exercise are concerned, nations are what count. It was even more so in 1914. During the previous four centuries, as even now in many parts of the world, a nation was what you wanted to be, the consummate glory of social aspiration. From 1914 to 1918, Europeans were to learn that this glory was so far intermixed with pain as to be glory no longer. Yet the love of being a nation survived—survived yet a second agony, survived (one may fear) to effect a final holocaust in which the nations fulfill their destiny by being destroyed.

Thus, as I look back through my lifetime to the sadly waving plumes and the malignant crossbones and the struttings of those dead and bastard potentates, I recall what I, too, felt. The feelings were boyish, but they were direct and pure, unencumbered by knowledge of any sort. You were, or you thought you were, attacked; somebody dared you to stand up for something. Standing up for something is a sign of manhood, which every boy wishes to attain. And so I can understand why Rupert Brooke, who, if he had not died in that war, might have made English poetry other than it is, wrote what now seems wildly mistaken: "Now God be thanked who has matched us with His hour. . . ."

Brooke's young Englishmen soon became the Old Contemptibles, and vanished at Mons and at the Marne. They had an ideal they guarded: the ideal of a nation at once safe and beneficent. Yet too great human suffering diminishes the ideal suffered for. Moreover, it became apparent, in time, that ideals had not been the only powers at work.

The youth were idealistically naïve. Their elders and rulers were naïve also, but not from ideals. Those hard-bitten statesmen, generals, diplomats, sophisticated by years of ruse and calumny, were naïve enough to trust their own sophistication. Germans put faith in the Schlieffen Plan, which they could not follow, and which perhaps would not have succeeded if they had followed it. The French had a fantasy that all would go well if only they attacked. Attacks by both sides failed, and the war became a siege in trenches. At the last, all ended, not so much by superior power as by the threat of revolution. The quarrels of commerce fell silent before the new historical event that commerce as a means of profit need not exist at all.

Before that war, some persons did perceive the character it would have. One of these, by a remarkable irony, was the sole man who had a chance at quick victory: Colonel-General Hellmuth von Moltke, who commanded the invasion of Belgium and France in 1914. Some years earlier, he had written to his wife his guess at the nature of any future war:

It will become a war between peoples which is not to be concluded with a single battle but which will be a long, weary struggle with a country that will not acknowledge defeat until the whole strength of its people is broken; a war that even if we should be the victors will push our own people, too, to the limits of exhaustion.[4]

---

[4] Quoted by Corelli Barnett: *The Swordbearers* (London: Eyre and Spottiswoode; 1963), p. 34.

It was a true insight, and it ate away at the Colonel-
General's morale as he saw events confirming it, until at
last he had to be retired with something like a nervous
breakdown. The war drew its peculiar horror, not alone
from pitting populations against populations, but from
pitting men against material. You walked, close-file in the
early days and even in the later, into a horizontal gust of
machine-gun fire. Shells, in their bursting, dismembered
you. Gas shriveled your lungs. The artillery barrage that
was to open a path for your advance, in fact made the
terrain more difficult. It would have all been more sensible and more merciful, if the sides had agreed to sit where
they were until time should show which of them would
starve. Then they could have declared winners and losers,
and have gone home to give their myths to poetry and
their plumes to parade.

No man in his senses, one might think, would pit
flesh against steel. But the peculiar conditions of that
war, though they allowed the various high commands to
be in their senses, did not allow them to do much that was
sensible. When criticism of the carnage has run its course,
one is still left with a belief that the fighting could have
been conducted in no other way.[5] Men, by their own
ingenuity (which indeed they bragged readily enough
about), had made themselves the prisoners of circum-

---

[5] In a book review in the journal *History Today* (February,
1968, p. 133) Mr. John Terraine points out three "central, dis-
agreeable truths about the 1914–1918 war. . . . The first is that
any war waged for high stakes between two more or less equally-
matched, powerful opponents is bound to be hard, bloody and
brutal. . . . Secondly, the entry of the masses into war lends it
an ideological content that increases the bitterness and the
brutality. Thirdly, by 1914, modern technology had found ways
to mobilize, arm, feed the masses for war, and transport them
to the battlefield; but had not yet surmounted the further problem
of moving them about easily on the battlefield."

stance. Their majestic control over events—for it was
this that the plumes and the crossbones and the high hats
celebrated—had brought them where control ceased and
everything they did was folly.

In 1916, at Verdun—a place where today the very
monuments show forth the grim, emaciate horror of that
battle—occurred the most famous and most awful of all
those contests between men and steel. A certain Lieuten-
ant Garaudy watched his regiment, or the remains of it,
come out of the fighting:

> First came [he wrote] the skeletons of companies
> occasionally led by a wounded officer, leaning on a
> stick. All marched, or rather advanced, in small
> steps, zigzagging as if intoxicated. . . . They said
> nothing. They had even lost the strength to com-
> plain. . . . It seemed as if these mute faces were
> crying something terrible, the unbelievable horror
> of their martyrdom.[6]

France was never the same after that, nor Europe
either. One more nudge by war, and power left Europe
forever, to settle with divided balance in the West and in
the East. Europe has always been a geographical append-
age. After many a long year, the tail has ceased wagging
the dog.

I I I

IF YOU GO THROUGH the volumes of *Mind*,[7] 1914–1918,
you will have the impression that no war was in progress
at all—though the *Hibbert Journal* was aware of it and

---

6 Quoted by Alastair Horne: *The Price of Glory* (London:
Macmillan and Co.; 1962), p. 188.
7 Then, as now, the premier philosophical journal in the
English-speaking world.

had some striking things to say. I remember also Professor Whitehead's saying once that, during the battle of the Somme, he and Samuel Alexander walked across London arguing metaphysical questions. Both these men well understood the gravamen of philosophy, and Whitehead, in recounting the episode, was teasing himself for irrelevancy.

Yet, as we know, there is always Russell in these affairs, just as there is never Moore. Though, as he said, "tortured by patriotism," he nevertheless opposed the war:

> As a lover of truth, the national propaganda of all the belligerent nations sickened me. As a lover of civilization, the return to barbarism appalled me. . . . I hardly supposed that much good would come of opposing the War, but I felt that for the honor of human nature those who were not swept off their feet should show that they stood firm.[8]

Some comfort he took in the society of Santayana, then at Cambridge, whose detachment from politics was always resolute and Olympian. Indeed, at the moment the Germans were approaching Paris—irresistibly, as it seemed—Santayana remarked to Russell, "I think I must go over to Paris. My winter underclothes are there, and I should not like the Germans to get them."[9] This much contempt for politics was impressive, but Russell did not share it. He went on to help organize the Union of Democratic Control (the somewhat mystifying name of a group against the war), and, after conscription came in, he served a prison term as conscientious objector. And indeed in his old age (1961) he again went to prison, this

---

[8] Quoted in *Memoirs of Lady Ottoline Morrell* (New York: Alfred A. Knopf, Inc.; 1964), p. 269.
[9] Ibid., p. 270.

time for one week, for participating in a demonstration against The Bomb.

Looking back upon those years, Russell must often have felt the satisfaction of having been right. Governments did lie, with such passion that the intent to lie was soon lost in a belief that the lies were true. Moralists can have no truck with this. War was, and is, barbarous, and it was right to make a stand for the honor of human nature. Yet, so various are human needs and ideals, so intricate our relations with one another, that very many men of entire honesty did, with entire trust in that honesty, just those things that Russell felt bound to condemn. Russell's version is only half the story, though it is more than half the moral account.

One difficulty with prolonged peace is that it may beget and sustain an atmosphere of triviality. People, it seems, need great feats to perform, labors and risks on behalf of ideals. The knight-errant spirit is in every noble breast. We see it now in our young people, who work, amid many perils, for peace and a better world. Perhaps we older folk can take some credit for having reared them, but I would not be surprised to find that this sort of gallantry is part of "human nature."

For let us consider. How long, may one suppose, will a round of tea parties, of Henley regattas, of hunting seasons and seasons of vacation beneath the southern sun—or, to the contrary, of hours in factories, shops, offices, mines—how long will these content, not the mere love of variety, but the love of ideals? Every ideal has its intrinsic charm, but its thrust upon us—indeed, its thrust into us—comes from the fact that it alone can produce a Cause. And a Cause is a large number of people striving all together to make an ideal a fact.

Now, a Cause has a very special effect upon its participants. It ennobles them, or at any rate makes them feel ennobled. They are doing, or think they are doing, something extremely valuable. They are thus important to mankind, and, so far as they know this or think it, they cannot fail to take pride in themselves. Nothing gives fulfillment like a Cause. Men who have missed Causes have missed fulfillment, and perhaps cannot know the littleness in which they have been left.

If in 1914 Russell found a Cause (and a true one) in the honor of human nature, various millions of other men found a Cause in the honor of human nature as manifested in the honor of nationhood. Accordingly, during the First World War, those nations that had a parliamentary system, though defective in itself and allied militarily with Tsarist autocracy (a most opprobrious word in those days) had something they might reasonably consider advantageous to mankind. For, however defective any example of that system might be, no other system would, or could, allow the will of large populations to be expressed. It takes very little adjustment to transform this notion into an ideal of freedom for all mankind.

Furthermore, whatever might have happened if a Tsarist Russia had shared an Allied victory, nobody could suppose that a German victory would have had the smallest libertarian effect. If history teaches any lessons, we ought to know by now that German dominance is grossly incompatible with the liberties of mankind. The legend to be seen in even the smallest towns of France—"fusillés par les Allemands"—and in other countries according to their languages—is evidence enough.

It is difficult not to think, therefore, that the young Englishmen, the young Frenchmen, and (after 1917) the young Americans who fought to prevent this—and you could prevent it only by fighting—were right to do what they did. At the same time, it seems that Russell was right in his humanitarian view, and that Debs and Lenin were right in their account of the odious economic motives and consequences of the slaughter.

We appear to be overwhelmed with contradictions, and perhaps should resign commentary. Yet this is exactly how the moral life is—a struggle, not alone of people, but of values. Moral problems are problems just because some value has to be lost in order that some other value can be gained. And we have to decide, given circumstances we did not produce, what greater value, most difficult to know, is worth the sacrifice of other values.

I V

WHAT WAS SAID TO BE a treaty of peace was signed at Versailles, in 1919, in the Galerie des Glaces, where, in 1871, the first German emperor had been proclaimed. Clemenceau, leaving the ceremony, was heard to say: "C'est une belle journée." Harold Nicolson, hearing this, said to Marie Murat: "En êtes-vous sûre?" "Pas du tout," she replied, being (says Nicolson) "a woman of intelligence."[10]

Of this same occasion Mr. Herbert Hoover later wrote, "I did not come away exultant."[11]

The problem of making peace had proved so far insoluble that the treaty itself prepared the ground for future war. The apparently victorious powers had differing needs and wishes, which conflicted with one another and with the idealism the war had generated. But above

---

[10] Quoted in Ferdinand Czernin: *Versailles, 1919* (New York: G. P. Putnam's Sons; 1964), p. 395.

[11] *Years of Adventure* (New York: The Macmillian Co.; 1952), p. 468.

all there was the problem of how to keep Germany paying
and poor without driving her into Bolshevism.[12]

The sea-blockade, maintained by the British Navy,
continued in force, and the Germans were more or less
starving. Yet the French wanted as reparations the gold
by which alone the Germans could buy food. Bolshevism
in Germany had already been a near thing: Bavaria, in
fact, had been briefly a socialist republic. Thus the Allied
statesmen found themselves enclosed within a strife of
historical forces. The satisfaction of certain material appetites, and even of patriotic hopes, would endanger and
might destroy the rule of the commercial classes over
those same nations and throughout the world.

Lord Keynes describes one meeting of the great
powers, at which this agony reached its height. The victim
of the scene was M. Klotz, a Jew, a banker, and a delegate
of France seeking reparations for his country:

> Never have I seen the equal of the onslaught with
> which that poor man [Klotz] was overwhelmed. Do
> you know Klotz by sight?—a short, plump, heavy-
> moustached Jew, well-groomed, well-kept, but with
> an unsteady, roving eye, and his shoulders a little
> bent in instinctive deprecation. Lloyd George had al-
> ways hated him and despised him; and now saw
> in a twinkling that he could kill him. Women and
> children were starving, he cried, and here was Mr.
> Klotz prating and prating of his "goold." He leant
> forward and with a gesture of his hands indicated
> to everyone the image of a hideous Jew clutching a
> money bag. His eyes flashed and the words came out
> with a contempt so violent that he seemed almost

---

[12] This has been splendidly and extensively documented
in Arno J. Mayer: *Politics and Diplomacy of Peacemaking:
Containment and Counterrevolution at Versailles, 1918–1919*
(New York: Alfred A. Knopf, Inc.; 1967).

to be spitting at him. The anti-Semitism not far below the surface in such an assemblage as that one, was up in the heart of everyone. Everyone looked at Klotz with a momentary contempt and hatred; the poor man was bent over his seat, visibly cowering. We hardly knew what Lloyd George was saying, but the words "goold" and "Klotz" were repeated, and each time with exaggerated contempt. Then, turning, he called on Clemenceau to put a stop to these obstructive tactics, otherwise, he cried, M. Klotz would rank with Lenin and Trotsky among those who had spread Bolshevism in Europe. The Prime Minister ceased. All around the room you could see each one grinning and whispering to his neighbor "Klotsky."[13]

Klotsky! With this word Lloyd George had formulated, and the assembled experts had received with grins, what later became Hitler's doctrine of "Jewish Bolshevism." For his part, M. Klotz was only behaving as a French patriot, who wanted the Germans to pay for the destruction they had wreaked in France. Anti-Semitism, "not far below the surface in such an assemblage" (assemblage! just two government chiefs and their advisers), would of itself have made those persons unfit for the conduct of any human affairs whatever. Whether bigotry had made them knaves or knavery had made them bigots, they were totally incapable of peace, even if circumstances had permitted peace.

And so, among the Allied nations, the heroes who had fought the battles came home to gloom and unemployment, the infinite market that war affords having disappeared. To be sure, in the mid-twenties, the United States had a period of prosperity. But when the dread

---

[13] *Two Memoirs* (London: Rupert Hart-Davis; 1949), pp. 61–2.

thirties began, every inhabitant of the West grew acquainted with the law of capitalism, that profit-making
by a few leaves the many unable to buy, and hence to
use, the goods they have themselves produced. The Great
Depression (it seems now to be capitalized) was in its
turn an agony almost as great as the war had been.

While these events were going forward, there developed in Vienna a philosophical school that discovered,
or perhaps rediscovered,[14] a safe mode of intellectual rebellion. This school had little to say that was genuinely
new, the main doctrines having been set forth by Berkeley
and Hume in 1710 and 1739 respectively. The school
called itself, or came to be called, the *Wienerkreis*, the
Vienna Circle, and it found a way to protect philosophy
from the police.

The theory was that we can know matters of fact,
such as whether the moon is full tonight, because we can
set up a test to verify the actual state of affairs: we can
go out of doors and look. But no test (so the theory ran)
can be set up to determine whether or not robbery, say,
is good or bad. If you try to find out whether robbery is
good or bad by using the sort of test that will tell you
whether the moon is full tonight, all you will find is that
a certain number of people dislike robbery—while at the
same time, no doubt, a certain number of other people
like it.

Tests tell you what is, but no test tells you what
ought to be. In this manner, ethical theory, which had
been reduced by Moore to a matter of private insight,
passed into the view that, although everything that science says is meaningful, nothing that ethics says has any
normative meaning whatever. There will be a tabulation
of preferences—of what people actually do prefer—and

---

[14] David Hume knew all this in the eighteenth century.

no more. Ethics sinks into sociology. And all the ruined bodies, the starving stomachs, cannot call their condition evil, but can only accept the liking or disliking of men as these chance to occur.

The rulers of the West, through the intellectuals who explain such things to them, received the theory of the *Wienerkreis* with quiet pleasure. They could not use it in ordinary politics, because it was far too sophisticated, and because most citizens regarded moral norms as meaningful and cogent. But during the 1930s, logical positivism (for so the theory was called) paralyzed much thinking and almost all action by intellectuals.

It was extremely difficult, for example, to get an intellectual to do anything about the starvation of his fellow men—his fellow Americans, indeed. You had first to convince him that starvation was a bad thing, and mass starvation worse. When you set out to do this, you at once encountered the positivist view (he had picked it up somewhere) that, although this or that person might dislike starvation, there was no way to demonstrate, and hence to *know*, that starvation was bad. Indeed, the simple sentence itself, "Starvation is bad," was held to be meaningless except when construed as "I don't like starvation" or "So-and-so doesn't like starvation."

The moral holiday thus declared was all too evident, and no one needed it more than the rulers themselves. Intellectuals got nothing from it but escape from commitment and a certain ease within their pitiful incomes. But the rulers, who had produced one holocaust, who had with their peace treaty prepared a second (as they are now preparing a third), were happy to be told that ethics contains no ideals to be striven for, no imperatives to be obeyed—rather, that all the sages of the past had uttered no more than a sigh of pleasure about this or a grunt of distaste about that.

Moreover, during the twenties and thirties, it became apparent that socialism was in the world to stay. The old theological riddle, "Why doesn't God kill the Devil?", seemed to find answer: He can't. Although Mr. Churchill proposed to strangle the Soviet infant in its cradle, the infant in fact behaved like Hercules with the serpents. By 1922, the question of recognizing the Soviet Government arose, and the British were ready to accept what they could not strangle.

There thus came a time, the Genoa Conference being set for mid-April, when King George V said to Lloyd George: "I suppose you will be meeting Lenin and Trotsky?" And Lloyd George replied: "Unfortunately, sir, I am not able to choose between the people I am forced to meet in your service. A little while ago I had to shake hands with Sami Bey, a ruffian who was missing the whole of one day, and finally traced to a sodomy house in the East End. He was the representative of Mustapha Kemal, a man who I understand has grown tired of affairs with women and has lately taken up unnatural sexual intercourse. I must confess I do not think there is very much to choose between these persons whom I am forced to meet from time to time in Your Majesty's service."

Lord Beaverbrook, who tells this story,[15] adds that "the King's only reply was to roar with laughter." Laughter is right enough, but on different grounds. Lloyd George was not quite in a position himself to jest about sexuality; but, beyond that, his doing so displayed (as those who remember the times will know) the extraordinary Freudian seizure that shook the bourgeoisie. The Bolshevik Revolution did indeed recover land and industry for the whole people, and the private owners of these were vastly dis-

---

[15] *The Decline and Fall of Lloyd George* (London: Collins; 1963), pp. 135–6.

tressed. Their vocal response, however, was founded not so much on property as on sex. Lenin, the most unprofligate of men, was said to have nationalized the corps de ballet for his own pleasure, and every husband throughout the West was warned that communism might confirm in his wife certain wishes she might be expected to have. A great social change, which touched upon sex only tangentially, was thus reduced to its tangent. It surprises me that Freud himself, who watched the whole occurrence, did not see, or at any rate did not say, that the bourgeoisie was complaining it had been screwed.

The Prime Minister, whose anti-Semitism had demolished the French patriot Klotz, and whose appetitive itch had equated socialism with sodomy, was, if not a fair sample, then at least *a* sample of the rulers of the West. He became in time an admirer of Hitler, and thus he marks one of the limits of Western liberalism. I do not know that he ever read one word of the positivist anti-ethic, but it seems fair to say that if he had been told that "good" means only "I like it," he would have felt even more at ease than he did.

V

FROM 1914 TO 1918, millions died by violence. From 1929 to 1938 (a year when the prospect of a new war restored "prosperity"), thousands starved and died. A vast failure of society was the most evident phenomenon in the West, together with a clear chance at recovery by popular effort at satisfying popular needs. Some Western powers, however, met the crisis by resorting to fascism.

What had the philosophical moralists to say during this time? They said, grounding themselves upon the *Wienerkreis*, that you could not *know* good or bad, right or wrong; you could only express your feelings. This theory of sighs and grunts we have already identified, supra, as Professor Ayer's, and have said that it belongs to the year 1936. Professor Stevenson's extension of the theory to include persuasion belongs, we have said, to the year 1937, when he published the first of three articles in *Mind.* The other two articles are from 1938. The emotivist theory was then supreme, and perhaps remains so still.

By 1938, however, the Nazis in Germany were beginning to show what an emotivist ethics could really do. On November 9–10, 1938, occurred the Crystal Night, when Jewish shops were shattered all over Germany. We know what happened after.

But one thing less well known is a remark the celebrated Eichmann made just before the Third Reich collapsed. As you read the text of the remark, keep in the front of your mind the meaning of the emotive theory: ethical statements express only our present feelings; one person's feelings cannot contradict another person's feelings; and, since we can't dispute about feelings, we can't dispute about ethics. Eichmann said to one of his friends that he "would leap laughing into his grave because the feeling that he had five million people on his conscience would be for him a source of extraordinary satisfaction."[16]

One strange phrase in this statement, "on his conscience," echoes an older and non-emotivist ethic. Eichmann's mother must have told him once that he had a conscience: he had no further acquaintance with it. What he said in the rest of the statement was that he had superintended the killing of five million people and that he had just loved it. It gave him "extraordinary satisfaction." That was his then present feeling. Is it really true, does one think, that we can oppose to him nothing but *our* present

---

[16] Shirer: *Third Reich.*, p. 1273 *n.*

feeling that this was horrible? Is there no rule, no norm, no thou-shalt-not, that we could have set between him and his victims?

Or, more alarmingly yet, since feelings change, and since the I-wish-you-would can become coercion, what is to prevent an emotivist from taking Eichmann's side? After all, Eichmann killed only five million people. It is now possible for an emotivist, if he becomes head of state in certain countries, to effect the annihilation of mankind. He will have gone underground for protection in doing this, and perhaps there will be a moment before the fire gets him when he too will feel extraordinary satisfaction. Yet, regardless of what he feels, will the annihilation of mankind have been a good thing?

This question restores our sanity, much weakened by the horror of events and the timidity of moralists. Since the survival of mankind is the precondition of every other good and even of the sighs and grunts of the emotivists, annihilation appears to be the ultimate evil. Yet it is some measure of our madness that the question can be asked at all, and that a leading philosophical school can say no more about it than "I like survival and I wish you would too"—especially when that same school can find no reason *not* to say: "I don't like survival and I wish you wouldn't either."

The last horror is perhaps too blinding an example, and will not let us see the specific error in the emotivist view. Fittingly enough, the error lies in a misreading of language. Consider, then, this calmer, indeed pedestrian, example:

An old proverb tells us that good instruction is better than riches. What shall we say this proverb means? One view (positivist but still sedate) would be that "Good instruction is better than riches" means "I would rather have good instruction than have riches." If, now, we relax this a little, as emotivists do, the meaning becomes "I get a bigger kick out of good instruction than I get out of riches." And on Stevenson's extension of emotivism the meaning becomes "I wish you'd get a bigger kick out of good instruction than you get out of riches." It is a millionaire talking to his son, forty years ago. No such conversation would happen now.

Yet the *fact* is that the proverb means none of these things at all. The proverb means that good instruction is to be preferred to riches, ought to be preferred to riches, no matter what anyone's preference happens to be. A man may not like good instruction, and, so far from getting a kick out of it, he may find it a dismal bore. The proverb tells him that he jolly well ought to prefer it anyway. Nor can that "ought" be reduced to an I-wish-you-would. For the proverb expresses a rule considered as binding upon every man's decision, so that, even though personally he may like riches much more than good instruction, we are made aware that he ought to decide the matter in just the other way.

Slaughter gave Eichmann extraordinary satisfaction. It was profoundly evil nevertheless. Annihilation of mankind may give some future emotivist extraordinary satisfaction. It will be, if it occurs, profoundly evil nevertheless. No one can make anything good by liking it nor evil by disliking it; nor can he make it good or evil by asking for assent or dissent. It is extraordinary (as was Eichmann's satisfaction) that such notions have been seriously proposed. I think, indeed, they would not have been, if they had not offered such agility of escape from personal commitment to solving the problems of our time.

4

Can I Know
What's Right?

THE MEN WHO ENDED ONE WAR in 1945 and began another in 1946 acted expectably. It would have been asking too much, not of human nature as such but of human nature as manifested in dominant classes, to have hoped or required abandonment of a new empire, an American empire, the largest yet. The rulers of America had appetites, which they readily construed as "commitments." They soon developed policies, which in turn they construed as the law of nations or of God.

The new empire was to be a work of salvation, and by it millions of men, regardless of their race, their color, or their wishes, were to be rescued from communism. About this time Congress inserted into the Pledge of Allegiance a phrase that had been notably absent before. Thus far, we had been "one Nation indivisible"; we were henceforth to be "one Nation under God." It was the acceptance of empire.

But suppose the choice of policy had been different. Suppose that, instead of replacing the old war with a cold war, of making deeper clefts in human affairs, of hanging above and across everything the threat of nuclear annihilation, these men had set about healing all wounds, joining with all other peoples in the effort, placing nuclear power at the service of mankind. Would we not be living in a fairer, safer, happier world?

It seems obvious that we would. It may also seem obvious that the fairer, safer, happier world would be a better world, a world we ought to try (as our rulers ought to have tried) to produce. I don't think our rulers gave that world much thought; it seemed perhaps too fanciful. Yet the choice was there, a perfectly real alternative to the choice made. Something like it lived briefly as UNNRA (the United Nations Relief and Rehabilitation Administration), and then expired. Something like it was the United Nations itself, which, however, soon became an instrument of American policy. The better world had twitchings as of life, but it was born dead.

Now, I suppose that some people would not regard my "better world" as better at all; indeed, they might think it worse than the world that has come in fact to be. And they would give reasons for their view (though not perhaps the reasons actually at work). They would say, perhaps, that a thoroughly peaceful world is more dangerous, as lacking sufficient resistance to communism. This would be what may be called a factual reason, since efficacy of resistance is a question of fact. To it would have to be added some other reason, explicitly ethical, in order to complete the grounds of choice. Such a reason might be that it is better to resist communism than to maintain peace in the world.

There is of course a leftwing view corresponding to this. Peace, it can be said, does not offer suitable conditions for resisting capitalism; and it is better to resist capitalism than to maintain peace.

I am not concerned here with the merit of either view. My concern is to show that both the views have a common pattern, which is characteristic of answers to problems of choice; and I have selected a problem that is momentous in the sense that the decisions made upon it will affect every man alive.

Thus, placing ourselves back in the years 1945–1946, we ask: ought the policy to be cooperation with the socialist world or ought it to be hostility, in the various degrees indicated by such terms as "containment" or "roll-back"? The second alternative was, of course, historically the choice; and a new phrase was coined for it, "Cold War"—presumably on the ground that, when it comes to war, some like it hot, but most like it cold.

American capitalists, seeing the world up for grabs and themselves as abundantly powerful, could not resist temptation. Nevertheless, they must have canvassed the matter among themselves and with their politicians. This would have involved, essentially, the giving of reasons why the choice was, if not wholly excellent, then at any rate valid. Perhaps "valid" meant nothing more than "we can get away with it." Still, there must have been at least a dim awareness that getting away with it, being able to do it, is a significant part of the grounds of choice.

The moral level of all this was not very high, and touched nothing so noble as the safety or even the survival of mankind. Nevertheless, the discussants must have satisfied themselves that they pretty well *knew* which choice was "preferable" or "better," within the meanings they were accustomed to give those terms. They didn't go by sighs and grunts or hortatory exclamations (though there may have been these). You don't employ advisers to supply you with grunts. No, the discussants went by reasons and arguments. Any other course is fatal in politics, a place where only the public may be passionate.

Equally, the leftwing view presents itself as founded upon knowledge. It would give, and indeed has extensively given, reasons and arguments why capitalism requires to be ushered out of history, why people who wish socialism are justified in trying to get it. Quite as capitalists with capitalism, socialists will say that they don't just *feel* socialism to be good, but that they *know* it to be good and can tell you why.

I I

TELLING WHY, giving reasons why, is an entirely familiar fact in the moral life. Everyone does it, and does it constantly. Not to do it would be as if a defendant, being asked why he committed the crime, were to answer, "I felt like it," or (if he possessed the positivist vocabulary) "I preferred." No judge or jury would take this to be justification.

Why do we so abundantly give reasons why? Well, for one thing, not to do so seems to diminish our humanity. There are, to be sure, times when we permit this or even require it. It was gallant of the Light Brigade not to "reason why," since battles apparently cannot be won if strategy is left to the individual soldiers. Yet the gallantry failed because someone had blundered. Somewhere, at some time, and by someone, there has to be a consideration of reasons, and the consideration may err.

But, ordinarily, a man is expected to be able to account for his actions, to give the reasons why he does what he does. For that matter, the members of the Light Brigade would have been entirely able to state the reasons why they didn't reason why. It was their duty not to: they were giving up the customary exercise of personal decision on behalf of what they took to be some greater value. A decision to let someone else decide is itself a decision, and will have its reasons too.

Apart from the demands of duty or of candor ("Let me explain to you why I am doing this"), the search for reasons and the assembling of them are essential to all conscious, deliberate acts of choice. Shall you marry at all, and, if so, shall you marry *this* person? Well, you must guess the future from the present, knowing, the while, that the guesses are only guesses. You must distinguish among the relevant values as to their exact nature and power, for the gaining of some of them will entail a loss of others, and you will want to make sure, so far as you can, that the lost values are the lesser.

All this material, gathered and organized, is the reason why. It stands, or seems to stand, to the ultimate decision as proof stands to the conclusion of an argument, as evidence to the thing inferred. It is, or seems to be, demonstrative. And a man who constantly founds his choices upon proof of this sort is a man whom we would call rational.

We have, accordingly, a strong disposition to regard ethics as one of the forms of human knowledge. It seems entirely familiar to say, "I know that good instruction is better than riches," or, alternatively, "I know I ought to prefer good instruction to riches." The assertions seem subject to demonstration, and, if I turn out to be mistaken, I am mistaken in much the same way as with any other erroneous view. The concept also exists in law: a defendant who does not know right from wrong cannot be tried, because he is considered to be not a moral agent, not responsible for his acts.

Again, it seems entirely familiar to say: "I don't know whether it would be better to marry Mabel or Jean" —"I don't know whether I ought to have voted for Johnson"—"I don't know whether I ought to take this risk." Every such assertion will evoke a further search for reasons, a further canvassing of them, in the hope that some one choice will be shown to be correct. This is what disputants on ethical questions think they are doing, even though Professor Ayer, as we have seen, assured them that they cannot.

There is still another respect in which ethics seems to be a form of knowledge. All knowledge is constituted of true assertions—assertions, that is to say, which express the state of affairs exactly as it is. Knowledge thus enables its possessor to deal with the state of affairs. The opposite of knowledge, ignorance or error, will not so enable him, and may leave him helpless. Thus, though we can regard knowledge as a vast series of sentences laid down in books, we can also think of it as a posture—the posture of a man able to deal with the world skillfully. If, for example, a man knows that his hat is in the hall closet, he can go there and get it. Knowledge has put him (I hope it is not pompous to say) in the posture of being able to deal with that small portion of the world.

Now, I think it can be said that ethics, as a form of knowledge, assists this sort of posture in a very intimate way. If a man is to deal with the world at all, he has to prefer dealing with it to not dealing with it; and if he is to solve his problems, he has to prefer solving them to not solving them. Now, he may be a man who has these preferences, so to say, by nature. Nevertheless, the question can be put to him, Why solve problems? Why deal with the world? He cannot escape inquiry into the grounds of his preference: the mere assertion "I prefer" has no such saving power.

Thus touched by inquiry, he would, as a rational man, try to demonstrate that it is better to deal with the world than not to deal with it, better to attempt solutions than not attempt them. Demonstrations would mean that he can *know* the one to be better than the other. Doubtless he would find that the demonstration was not definitive, and that the argument had vulnerable edges. But demonstration would gain cogency as it gained breadth, and he would end by thinking: "Well, this is very probably the case" or "I'm pretty sure that this is so." This state is also

one we are in with regard to many assertions of the
sciences—notably, for example, those concerning the
origin of life or of the universe. The "edges" of ethics are
speculative, but so also are those of the sciences.

For human beings, choice, decision, is an essential
part of the posture of dealing with the world. It would be
extremely odd if the case were such that we know the
world but not know any grounds for making choices.
For we would then not know the one thing without which
the rest of knowledge would be mostly useless. We would
be in the state—well, we *are* in it, we who live in the West
—of knowing how to kill everybody on earth, but not
knowing that we oughtn't. The soulless scientists with
their "value-free" sciences, the "objective" historians who
take no side (except that of the Establishment), know, it
may be, something of the world; but values, duties, mer-
cies, ideals are not part of that knowledge, are perhaps
not matters of knowledge at all. They would like to think
this, they would like to have it proved or at least supported
by argument. It was they whom positivism succored in
their agony, they for whom emotivism was balm. For a
government grant is a thing to live on; and living's not
living if you know that your choice has made you a killer,
not of this man or that, but of millions, perhaps billions,
by detonation, suffocation, strangulation, or the wily
ingress of germs.

People—of certain sorts at least—have their reasons
for wanting not to know reasons, for wanting reasons not
to be known, and for wanting certain things to have no reasons. If, for example, decisions have, and can have, no reasons, nobody at all can be accountable for what he decides.
If he were to be accountable, reasons would have to be
adduced as to why he is so. But if choices have no ground,
no reasons—are, consequently, not matters of knowledge

—then every chooser is free. Free? Free to like and prefer, to "evince" liking and preference, and to perish in his choices along with us all.

I I I

THE PRESTIGE OF SCIENCE in any culture that can call itself advanced leaves us quite unable to doubt that knowledge of fact is indeed knowledge. The world is out there, all around us. We extensively describe that world, and, so far as our descriptions correspond with the world, they are true and are matters of knowledge. But the old nagging awareness that fact isn't necessarily value, that what is isn't necessarily what ought to be, keeps on suggesting that whatever is normative in ethics—the ideals, standards, rules—are perhaps not matters of knowledge at all. This notion, as I have just now observed, supports much lethal activity by people who would rather not think themselves lethal. The notion therefore assists, promotes, self-serving apologetics. One may suspect that the notion is in fact corrupt. What is mainly required is, however, that the notion be shown to be false. For if it is in fact true, we shall just have to accept it, and let the self-servers revel in success.

There always is the possibility that nothing good can come of it all, that the villains, sycophants, and mere gross instruments of evil have the thing sewed up. I think they don't—that, quite to the contrary, their sins, accumulating, will be their ruin. I a little regret the probable result, namely, that the "value free" scientists and the "objective" historians will, when the better world comes, swiftly make themselves valueful and partisan. They have the souls of willing employees, and for them the better world won't seem any different from the bad one.

They may keep their ineluctable level, then, but I must try to show why their present solace is false solace. I must give reasons why we can *know* that this or that is good or bad, right or wrong, ought to be done or ought not to be done.

The notion that the sciences are "value-free" gains some strength from the fact that the more exact (are they so?) sciences, the ones that have delivered the physical world into our hands, seem to have no moral content whatever. There *seems* nothing to be found about ethics in chemistry, physics, astronomy. These sciences are models of the knowledge of what is, and they *seem* silent about what ought to be.

But these are not the only sciences there are. Physical scientists, to be sure, lord it over social scientists, as if mathematical exactitude gave them some special unction. The social sciences are sciences for all that: they try to state what is the case, and do in fact sometimes state it. There are veracious histories and historians. Sociologists are able to say a good deal of what is true about society, economists about the economy, psychologists about people.

In all these disciplines, however, questions of value keep turning up as part of the material, even when the practitioners warmly assert that their sole task is to describe, not recommend. For how is one to describe anything human without evoking the question whether the phenomenon described is as it ought to be? A description of business cycles ("boom to bust") suggests all too plainly that there could be better social arrangements. A dispassionate history of the American Blacks (if indeed one could be written) would not suggest, but proclaim, the iniquity of their sufferings. In fact, governments and other social establishments tamper with these sciences all the time, in order to make the findings justify policy or at least not condemn it.

And there is one science, psychotherapy, which seems to have ethics as part of its essence. The cure this science seeks to effect, and does quite often effect, has to do with the psychological grounds of rational decision. The patient discovers what his actual motives are, how he came to have them, and what the environment really is in which he expresses them. In this way, he learns to identify all sorts of mistakes and the wrong choices they lead to.

I suppose that no psychoanalyst faithful to the precepts of his craft will tell a patient what that patient ought to do. It is part of therapy to obey the maxim of Lady Macbeth's doctor: "Therein the patient/ Must minister to himself." In all this, however, there is a clear assumption that psychological health is *better than* psychological illness, and that any rational man *ought to* prefer it. There is a further assumption that psychological health lies in *knowing* the actual state of affairs and the values connected with it: illusions, however attractive, are dangerous and ought to be dispelled.

Psychotherapy assumes, therefore, that there are right conditions and wrong conditions for making choices. We have only to add that there are right choices which right conditions tend to make possible, and wrong choices which wrong conditions tend to make possible, and we find we have entered ethics itself.

If, now, we look back over all the sciences thus reviewed, then perhaps the "natural" sciences will seem less grimly non-moral than is sometimes supposed. For if, as we said, a description of business cycles immediately suggests their foolishness, the physical formula $E = mc^2$ now suggests catastrophe. Or again, as geneticists approach being able to determine in advance what sort of children shall be born, the question will rise, ever more insistently: What sort (or sorts) of people ought there to be? We observe at once that, if the question does not reach the level of "ought" but is left in the pre-moral level of "What kinds of human beings are in fact wanted?" the effective answers will come from men of present power, and the children then scientifically produced will be predestined to docility.

All knowledge is either presently useful or able to become so. Usefulness always evokes the moral question about what uses ought to be served. It would be odd, and indeed most frustrating, if we could know the knowledge and the uses, but not know the "ought." For we would then be baffled at the very heart of decision, and we would waste upon mere accident of appetite or social pressure our hard-won psychological health.

I V

THIS SAD STATE may, however, be the one we are in. We cannot reject the possibility merely because it would inconvenience us. We can reject it only after we have shown that there are, and can be known to be, ideals and standards and rules. Most people, I fancy, think there are. Some few happy sinners—by no means all sinners or all members of government—think there are not. The thing itself is not at all easy to prove; consequently, the happy sinners have a happier time of it than seems reasonable.

One line of argument might be, and indeed has been, that values are in the world just as anything else existent is in the world. Values, it can be said, are discoverable under certain conditions, in certain areas of space, and at certain moments of time. All these occur whenever a human need encounters a means of satisfaction. The means of satisfaction then has value, is valuable. A dinner on a table (assuming it to be nutritive and non-poisonous) is, uneaten, potentially valuable. When the hungry diners sit down, it actually has value. And it keeps on being valuable while the diners eat it and digest it and maintain their health with it.

So far we have nothing that is not knowable. The elements of the meal are knowable; so also is the hunger of the diners (their need for food) and the ability of the meal to satisfy it. So also is the value of the meal—the value being just that ability to satisfy a need. But we still have not reached the more difficult level, peculiar to ethics, where rest the ideals, the standards, the rules.

I don't suppose that even a gourmet would regard eating as an ideal, and, if he did, a psychiatrist would suspect him at once of oral dependency. There can be, perhaps, such a thing as an ideal dinner, but this would merely be a dinner that is very good for a dinner. Eating, as such, seems to be more like a necessity and a pleasure than an ideal.

Brotherhood, however, does seem to be an ideal. So also do peace, self-mastery, the creation of beauty, the possession of truth. What makes the difference between all these and being fed, clothed, housed? Why does it appear that food, clothing, and housing, though they satisfy needs essential to survival, stand as mere tributaries to the ideals? Why is it the case that man cannot live by bread alone?

One reason may be the peculiarity of the relation between means and ends. Although, as I think, the moral evaluation of any means involves a lot more than the merit of the end it serves, there is no doubt that the merit of the end *is* important to the evaluation. It seems not to be the case that the end justifies the means: far too many crimes have been committed on this notion. But it

does seem to be the case that the end contributes, sometimes decisively, to the justification of the means.

Now, things that are momentarily ends often turn
into means for something else. When you sit down to
today's dinner, your purpose (end) is to eat it. Once eaten,
the dinner becomes a means to your health and survival.
Your health and survival will no doubt remain ends for
you so long as you have either. But they are also, ad-
ditionally, means. They are means to further accomplish-
ments of all sorts, among which may be contributions you
will make to society.

It can happen, though it does not necessarily happen, that this flow of means into ends and of ends into
means widens as it proceeds. Some things you do give
satisfaction to more than one need at the given time. The
meal, for example, is not only a device for appeasing
hunger; it is a social institution, which satisfies also the
need for companionship, for love, for acceptance and approval by family and friends. Indeed, eating by oneself
is a kind of bereavement. Macaulay, a lifelong bachelor,
used to read a book while he ate; Mme du Deffand, who
was blind, had a servant read to her at meals. The book
substitutes for the person.

As the flow widens, as successive ends satisfy ever
more needs and, turning into means, lead on to still
larger satisfactions, we approach ideals. Brotherhood, the
whole human race in harmony, is one of these: it is a
state of affairs, now alas imaginary, in which the question, Whose need shall I satisfy? could be answered with
entire ease. Self-mastery, the skill of right decision, is
also an ideal: a state of character, not altogether imaginary, in which a man knows how to answer the question:
Which need shall I satisfy?

The widening of the flow may be seen in another
way. When a man satisfies some of his needs by food,

clothing, shelter, he behaves as a consumer. Such behavior is important, though advertising exaggerates the importance by pleading for more consumption than there can be. Men, however, are not consumers only. They are producers, too—and not merely in order to consume the products. Quite like beavers, men have a need to play around with the environment, making things, doing things. Gross inactivity is neurotic and will cause gross unhappiness. The old theology was not wrong to list sloth among the seven deadly sins.

Thus it seems that we need to make things as well as consume them, to give as well as get. A supposed ideal which magnifies only one of these activities is much too limited, is really not an ideal at all. We may therefore infer that, in the course of a lifetime, the satisfaction of needs ought to occur in such a way as to develop the whole person and the main attributes of humanity in that person. By this notion I don't quite mean what is sometimes called well-roundedness, as if we were to become spheres rolling about the world. Rather, I mean that each of us is to be the particular modification of humanity that he historically is, and he may tend to this or that exaggeration of the basic material. Yet his life ought to show creativity as well as consumption; moreover, social relations ought to be arranged so as to allow some ease in both. Thus in the concept of the whole person and that of a harmonious society we have two ideals, which are, in their essence, probably one.

No doubt ideals, since we must see them from a distance, remain a little shadowy. The broadening river flows into an ocean we can never quite chart, and all we have are "murmurs and scents of the infinite sea." Nevertheless the ideals seem to have some sort of authority; they not only beckon, they command pursuit. I have the idea that they get this authority from expressing what may be called entirety or perfection. Thus they surpass our limited satisfactions, and make us aware in the possession of little things how much we have still to gain.

All these matters, so far as I can tell, are known or knowable. There may be doubt whether authority and perfection are connected in the way I have described, but this seems a doubt which further inquiry can settle one way or the other. I don't find in it anything radically resistant to inquiry. In all human inquiry, when reason has done its best, something still remains unknown; but this, I think, is due to the frailty of our powers, not to intractability in the subject.

V

IDEALS WILL SERVE, ethically, as standards of conduct. Hence, so far as ideals are knowable, standards are knowable too. We have now to ask whether the same thing holds for rules.

Now, rules are directives: they tell us what to do, and sometimes also where and when to do it. Grammatically, they use verbs in the imperative mood: "Do as you would be done by." Also they are general in the sense that they apply to an indefinite number of cases. Even if you modify a rule to allow for special circumstances, the rule thus modified retains a general import. To take an example that casuistry has long made stale: if you modify the rule "Don't tell a lie" so as to exempt occasions when you want to mislead and thus defeat a criminal, you are still left with a rule of general import, namely, "Go ahead and lie whenever these circumstances occur."

What may be called technological rules derive from statements of fact, and they exist because we know enough about the world to be able to control certain events within it. Recipe rules, for example: "Bake for 90 minutes at 350°." This rule derives from our knowledge that that degree of heat and extent of time will have that effect upon that kind of batter.

Game rules are slightly different. They are, I suppose, constructed upon certain facts, particularly facts related to human skills. Further, the rules must make a genuine contest possible; otherwise they don't provide a game, any more than loaded dice provide a game. Beyond this, they are quite arbitrary. We can say that the players "must" observe them; but by this we mean that if the players observe the rules, the game will be the genuine game it is, and if not, not.

Does the "must" mean only that? Suppose we have a player who cheats. He is doing something the rules forbid, and is doing it for personal victory. He intends to achieve against the rules what he has not skill enough or luck enough to achieve within the rules. There is also an area, more black than gray, where players do things not expressly forbidden, but contrary to the spirit of the game.

Well, now: our imaginary cheat has broken one or more rules of the game, but these broken rules were not moral rules; they were only rules of the particular game, and were arbitrary to boot. *They* cannot condemn him. But perhaps there is a rule that can, expressible in the form "Thou shalt not cheat," or, less biblically, "Don't cheat." This rule is a rule of ethics, and by it violators are morally condemned.

The difference between a game rule and a moral rule is striking enough, although the two sometimes overlap. In some games, such as football and basketball, rule-breaking brings penalties within the game itself. Apparently, the notion is that any advantage gained by rule-breaking ought at once to be counterbalanced by loss within the play and texture of the game. This "ought" is at least in part a moral "ought"; that is to say, rule-breaking unpunished within the game would confer so much advantage that the game would not be the game it purports to be.

A somewhat similar condition holds in the vexed question of law and morality. What does one do about a statute which is iniquitous and which one knows to be iniquitous? The question assumes (what we have already asserted) that no statute has *moral* validity just by being a statute. Indeed, it may not even have legal validity. Where there is constitutional government, statute law must conform to the constitution, that is to say, to the basic law; beyond that, it will be possible to pursue both statute and constitution into the refinements of jurisprudence, the theory of law in general.

In some ways, statute law resembles the rules of games. It is somewhat arbitrary (though jurisprudence tries to get beyond this fact), and it prescribes what in general the people who live under it (the "players") are to do or not do. Its arbitrariness lies in the fact that it has been enacted or decreed. The men who enacted or decreed a certain law may have thought it morally valid and yet have been mistaken. Or they may have been quite consciously self-seeking and tyrannical. The human race has had rich and varied acquaintance with both sorts.

Thus there appear to be moral rules applicable to statute law and (more interestingly, perhaps) to lawmaking and law enforcement. One such rule is carved upon the Supreme Court Building in Washington: EQUAL JUSTICE UNDER LAW. For it is repugnant to morality that anyone in such circumstances should be put at a disadvantage. Law would then cease to be genuine law, just as games that permit rule-breaking would cease to be genuine games.

So far as the world of fact is concerned, the outward

and visible sign of authority is the imposition of sanctions. The game rule, the enacted law, get themselves enforced. Someone there is (a judge, a jury, a policeman, an umpire, a referee) to penalize violators for their violations. Something of this sort, indeed, has already existed in the relationship between parents and children, with not always happy results. At any rate, most of us will have grown up and lived our lives with a respect for rules and for laws —and, if we are candid about our humanity, with a certain amount of rebelliousness toward both.

It is not hard to recognize authority in these forms. But none of these forms is the form of *moral* authority. Any one of them—the law, the lawmaker, the law enforcer, the umpire, the parent—may be mistaken or even corrupt. But moral authority (if there is such a thing) cannot be either mistaken or corrupt. Quite to the contrary, it must be pure and infallible.

During past ages, as I conjecture, the sense that moral authority must be pure and infallible has combined with human experience of human authority to shape the idea of God. Our parents punished us for rule-breaking; the law punishes us for law-breaking; and there is a good deal of impromptu, extralegal punishing (or, at any rate, penalizing) by people who have the power and the wish (they usually have the wish if they have the power). We also grow aware that punishment for one infraction tends to deter us from others, and we surmise that this effect happens with everyone else. While all this is going on, we also discover fallibility, and even wickedness, among those who punish us. Our inference is not that punishment is improper for sin but that it ought not to be administered by sinners or fools.

We thereupon suppose (if I am guessing correctly) that our problem would be solved and the whole world made right, if there existed a supremely authoritative personage, perfect in power, in purity, and in knowledge. Such a personage would be God, and, thus constituted, he couldn't possibly fail to know what's right, to prefer what's right, and to do what's right.

Unfortunately, this concept yields exactly the inference that Leibniz drew: ours must be the best of all possible worlds.[1] To accept any such notion as this, we have to think out of existence the thousand stupendous evils that do exist, or we have somehow to think that they are not evils. In short, we cannot believe that there is any such God, without abandoning either our good sense or our good will.

It will be possible, of course, to say that God is perfect in knowledge and in preference, but not in power. Then we can say that evil is in the world because God cannot prevent it, though he would like to. But this loss or limitation of power scars the whole idea. An authoritative personage, who cannot do all that he knows is right, seems not supremely authoritative.

V I

THESE ARGUMENTS are old, hoary indeed, labored and beaten into clarity, and left to us now as mere exercises in logic. They have just that relation to the world which would exist if one debated whether a lady's complexion is of milk or of cream. The thing is poetry, not science. The concept of God is a metaphor that displays the human conscience grappling with moral problems, particularly with the problem of rules and their validity. We are alone in the universe so far as this is concerned. Morality is from first to last a human affair; yet it is rigorous and is not determinable by human whim.

---

[1] *Monadology,* § 55: "His goodness makes Him choose it, and His power makes Him produce it." Latta's translation.

We are thus left to do the right thing (if we do it) solely because it is right. There is no supernatural power to reward us for doing it or to punish us for not doing it. Indeed, we often enough see the wicked prosper and the righteous grieve. Indeed, there are people in the world whom the mere sight of innocence or excellence rouses to a fury of destruction: they seek to banish what is for them a constant reproach.

Virtue, then, is likely to suffer just because it evokes retaliation. We cannot expect any gains from it, still less "rewards"—though something of the kind may happen. But, then, gains and rewards—and punishments too —are morally irrelevant. Right is the sole reason for doing; it does not need, and in fact repels, the extraneous lure of personal gain. In this respect, the world as it is, with all its evils, is more of a moral economy than a theistic system of rewards and punishments would be.

Rewards and punishments are childhood stuff; the carrot and the club are for donkeys. Setting them aside, we can finally ask the question: What makes moral rules binding upon our choices, so that we can say we ought to apply them whether we want to or not?

The merely psychological ground is plain enough. People do have consciences and therefore have the feelings that "ought" and "should" suggest. Whether conscience is a physiological organ or a psychological organ ("superego") I do not know. But I am not here concerned with the feelings in the person. I am concerned with the authority in the rule.

Some of this authority, I believe, lies in the fact that all rules are general and ultimate rules are altogether universal. For example, there cannot be an ultimate rule that allows me exemption from moral rules as I may happen to wish. Nor can there be a rule that requires other people to do what I am not required to do in the same circumstances. Every rule of this sort would be self-contradictory, and hence not a rule. There is no such thing as special privilege in morality. Ethics is the great equalizer.

Further, it seems that if we are all equal in respect of being bound by rules, we must also be equal in respect of being served by them. If there cannot be special privilege in exemption, there cannot be special privilege in benefit. We are therefore to think, exactly as Kant said, that everyone deserves to be treated as an end, as worth doing things for. This notion is perhaps too individualistically expressed. We can complete it by saying that the welfare of mankind—that vast and tumultuous body of persons to which we all belong—is the source of authority for our moral rules.

This is the most I find myself able to say on the subject. Well, then, can it be said that what I have stated as the ultimate principle can be *known* to be ultimate? I would say, probably yes. I am aware that I have not put the principle beyond all doubt or question, but the argument tending toward it seems strong. One is driven from alternatives by their unreasonableness. For there cannot be an ultimate rule that allows exemption; and a ruleless ethics, without norms or standards, supplies no means whatever for making up one's mind.

I add, however, a cautionary note. The emotivist theory was shocking in its day, not only because it seemed to demolish traditional views, but because it sapped the moral strength, the zeal, required for the struggle against fascism. In the midst of great horrors it piped a thin voice. One therefore expected an emotivist to be wary of commitment, and this expectation was pretty well borne out.

If the emotivist theory has any moral frailty (aside from that of being unable to explain anything), that frailty would be detachment, aloofness from human affairs. The cognitive theory has tended to escape this, for people who are confident that they know right and wrong are usually involved. We must now admit, however, that the cognitive theory *may* lead to things that are less like frailty and more like vice. The great horrors of this century have been perpetrated by cognitivists, people who were sure they knew right and wrong. The Nazis, thinking (as they liked to say) with their blood, thought they knew all about the Jews. White supremacists think they know all about the Blacks. The rulers of the nuclear powers think they know all about "enemies." And there we are!

On the whole, I suppose, the aloof do mankind less harm but also less good than the committed, the skeptics than the convinced. Nevertheless, morality requires commitment, and asks us to have some confidence in our moral knowledge. But perhaps, even so, it will be well if skepticism, creeping back, softens from time to time our commitment with hesitation and our knowledge with doubt.

5

Love and
Self-Love

*T*HIS FLOWER opening to the sun; this weed dwindling
to the dark; this weed and flower. This angel-animal; this
spirit-beast; this much-loved *I.*

Love for others comes a little late perhaps; yet it
is early. It first came like an unfelt air, breathing toward
the breast we lay on, where we fed and were safe. It came
again, more like lightning, when we saw and knew

Woman is

That not impossible She
That shall command my heart and me. . . .

But the suddenness of these feelings—the infant trust,
the youthful rapture—was owing to needs satisfied, needs
of the fretful, striving self. One begins life needing another breast; one pursues life needing another body; one
ends life needing nothing at all.

Needs satisfied by others cause us to love others.
We seem, however, to need no such satisfaction in order
to love ourselves. This love, it would appear, we brought
with us from the womb, and perhaps within the womb it
was the theme of our dark meditations. There, in the
blind warmth, we had but to feed and grow. We have
not since been so prosperous or content. We did not then
know that our destiny was to pass from having everything
to having nothing, and we must have thought ourselves
laureates of success.

It was a true insight that led our forefathers to respect the past, to think that things had once been perfect: Adam before the fall, Eden before exile. The womb was this perfection, the embryo doing easily what it ought, the environment instantly satisfying needs. We may rejoice to know that, however we fare in life, there was a time when we and things alike were worthy of all praise. We needed no ethics, for we had no problems. And then, suddenly, helplessly, catastrophically, we were born.

We were born, not necessarily out of love, but with it. Thinking back, we cannot find a time when we did not love ourselves with a passionate and, it may be, a sacrificial love. There were no doubt moments, perhaps periods, of shame or shyness or discontent with the self. We couldn't run fast, or couldn't leap high, or couldn't learn quickly, or couldn't excel; and the world scratches these sores by its habit of offering praises and prizes. Yet, through all the shame and shyness and discontent, there endured the sympathetic love with which the loser wrapped his losses, turned them into treasures for memory, and thus made himself able to survive.

Self-love begins with the body, and never leaves it. We rejoice over every nerve and fibre, every cell and corpuscle, every nail and hair, every odor indeed. If manufacturers and their puffers were wise, they would, instead of deodorizing us, depilating us, and turning our aspect into something else again, confirm rather the much-loved existing fact. Our natural wish is to love straight hair, if we have that; to love curly hair, if we have that; to love our coloration as it is. Our shape and posture, too. How comes it that men, for mere profit, may intrude upon this contentment, and bring our self-love to dote on things unnatural?

Well, because self-love labors to find confirmation

in the approval of others. The same destiny that made us private made us also social. We wish to be like others, or at least not very different, in ideas, in behavior, and in loyalty to prevailing norms. Even non-conformists (as they seem now to be called) conform to established patterns of non-conformity, and lament with common voice how sad it is to be alone. Thus, since we are social beings, there are modes and fashions of doing things. These change, no doubt, it being always necessary to sell new commodities; but the changes occur in the mass, with society following each shift of direction like coils of a giant snake.

The working of self-love towards its contrary has been observed often enough. La Rochefoucauld thought this a sort of conspiracy in which everyone is helplessly engaged. Self-love, he said,

> exists in all states of life and all conditions. It lives everywhere and on everything; it lives on nothing. . . . It even goes over to the side of those who make war upon it. It enters into their designs, and (what is astonishing) it joins them in hating itself. It begs to be ruined; it labors to be destroyed. In the end, it cares solely about existing, and on behalf of this it is quite willing to be its own enemy.[1]

From this account La Rochefoucauld drew a series of celebrated inferences, which are highly cynical because highly moralized. The facts of human nature are somewhat (though by no means altogether) as he stated them, but they are facts merely. What gives the epigrams their sting is the ethics by which the facts are judged. There is an assumption, never quite acknowledged, that self-love is nasty: it can be profoundly vicious, and at best it will be shameful.

---

[1] *Maximes*, 563.

The immediate source of this notion was Christian pessimism—the belief that the original sin had been Adam's pride, his rebellious self-assertion. This flaw of character, this moral fault, he had bequeathed to his descendants, all men on earth, and had given them thus the lifelong problem of mastering self-love by practice of humility. Accordingly, La Rochefoucauld, a faithful communicant, left certain devout sayings among the cynical: "Humility is the true test of Christian virtues,"[2] or again, "Humility is the altar on which God desires us to offer sacrifice."[2]

But this dark view, though familiar, is not the only one there can be. A hundred years after La Rochefoucauld, the men of the Enlightenment regarded humility as a falsification of human merit and a crippling of human powers. We may perhaps wish to set aside, as extreme, the romantic notion of Rousseau that men are naturally good. There remains, however, his admirer, the sage of Koenigsberg, Immanuel Kant, whom no one can suspect of indifference to morality or religion. In a passage of more than ordinary vigor, Kant denounced such precepts as would make us "incapable of all respect for the worth of humanity in our own person and for the rights of men,"[3] and, equally, "that false humility which sets the only way of pleasing the Supreme Being in self-depreciation, in whining hypocritical repentance and in a mere passive state of mind."[3] According to this doctrine, men have so much moral worth, just by being men, that they need not and ought not abase themselves before any power whatever.

If we can feel this idea as well as hold it, we shall

---

[2] Ibid., 358 and 537 respectively.
[3] *Critique of Judgment,* Part I, § 29. Bernard's translation. It is said that the only picture in Kant's house was an engraved portrait of Rousseau.

be much less prone to those other feelings, nagging and negative, which are of guilt. I suppose it would be undesirable to lose those feelings altogether; if we did, we could not enjoy La Rochefoucauld. The epigrams play upon our feelings of guilt, and we laugh because they have released the tensions. As for the truth of their content, factual or moral, we can test that by turning them around. For example, instead of "Our virtues are for the most part only disguised vices," let us put "Our vices are for the most part only disguised virtues." An interesting case can be made for this, if we are willing to think of vices as actions done in excess. La Rochefoucauld's version pretty much reduces virtue to vice; my turnabout suggests that vice may be lifted to reveal virtue.

Perhaps, in the end, it was Pascal who had the thing best (indeed, in my view, he had almost everything right): our place in nature (somewhere between the infinitely small and the infinitely great), the kind of animal we are, the endowment we have, the pulse and drive of our wishes, the collisions to which they lead—all these establish and celebrate "la grandeur et la bassesse de l'homme." "It is dangerous," wrote Pascal, "to insist upon man's animality without showing him his grandeur. It is more dangerous to insist upon his grandeur without showing him his baseness. It is still more dangerous to ignore them both."[4]

In this odd, uncertain, itching state, we may use a device that Pascal, I dare say, would not quite have approved. If our animality is complained of, we can point to our grandeur; if our grandeur chances (though rarely) to be praised, we can be modest enough to say that we are animals after all. No doubt La Rochefoucauld, with his "esprit d'un singe," will tell us that "rejection of praise

---

[4] *Pensées*, 418.

is a wish to be praised twice," and the weightier Dr. Johnson will suggest that "censure of self is oblique praise." Nevertheless, we are ourselves, though rather too much embarrassed about it, and we will love the animal that is this spirit and the spirit that is this animal.

I I

No DOUBT we do the other species much wrong when we use the word "animal" to signify baseness. It appears, for example, and we are so told, that rats and men are the only species practicing fratricide. Wolves kill, but usually not one another. Tigers kill, but not one another. Lions . . . bears . . . and so on. There are, to be sure, contests within these species leading toward death, but the death does not happen. There comes a moment, just before the end, when the loser publicly admits that he has lost: the vanquished wolf offers his throat to the victor, who, however, does not bite.[5]

With rats and men the case is different. Their internecine strife is deadly, and, as I imagine, only the weakness of rattish intelligence has kept that species from destroying itself, to the defeat of commercial exterminators. The human species, having much higher intelligence, knows precisely how to destroy itself. The discoverers of this knowledge and the technologists of its use are therefore clearly superior to rats. All would perhaps be well, if it were not for the fact that other intelligences have scurried or crept into positions of power, where, with a certain dimness of mind, they think that war is peace.

Or so we infer from what they say. Perhaps, how-

---

[5] Konrad Lorenz: *On Aggression* (New York: Harcourt, Brace & World; 1966), p. 132.

ever, they don't really think that war is peace. Perhaps what they really think is that they are willing to have peace provided they can also have certain other things: raw materials, markets, cheap labor, and no powerful competitors. Probably it is easier, or more acceptable, for them to say that they are fighting for peace rather than profits. But if all this is true, then fighting doesn't occur for the love of fighting, is not an end in itself. Rather, it is a means to other ends. It seems to be the fact that our rulers do prefer power and profits to slaughter. Were the case otherwise, politics would be even more nonsensical than it is.

Accordingly, if, taking the facts, we are to draw generalizations about animal nature or human nature, we cannot conclude that animals and people kill, cheat, and rob because they have a primal need to kill, cheat, and rob. People and animals (when they are sane, at any rate) kill, cheat, and rob only on behalf of quite different ends. A man who thought he was committing a crime for its own sake, or for the sake of its criminality, would be profoundly deluded. Any psychoanalyst could tell him that the crime and the fact of its being a crime attracted him because they satisfied entirely different motives— motives, indeed, which, if they had been rationally satisfied, would have caused no harm.

We are therefore *not* so constituted that we must kill, cheat, rob; but we are so constituted that we must try to live, and try to achieve, and try to love. This seems to me to be the bare and basic fact. It is nevertheless the case that, in trying to live and achieve and love, people find themselves willing to do all kinds of harm—to one another obviously, but also, less obviously, each to himself.

"Aggressiveness"—the constant assertion of the self and its needs and wishes—does no doubt appear in everything we do; the alternative would be a gross, disastrous passivity (which, I suppose, would turn out upon analysis to be another mode of trying to get what one wants). This "aggressiveness" meets an environment, a system of relations in nature and society, which allows, or frustrates, the passage of the self toward its goals. If the environment is favorable, Little Jack Horner eats his pie and remarks upon his own excellence. If the environment is unfavorable, Little Jack Horner tries to go ahead anyway, wrestling with obstacles, possibly overturning them, leaving behind the traces of his power if not of his excellence. It will be true to say that his aggressiveness contributes to the result, but the circumstances in which he acts contribute also. Indeed, they contribute more. They are older than he; they are vaster and more powerful. Struggle as he may, he cannot do much more than "adapt."

Now, all our generalizations about human nature have to be derived from observed or recorded instances of what people do in fact do. Not one of these observed and recorded instances exhibits any person whatever in total independence of the circumstances he acts in. Accordingly, we have, and have long had, theories that attribute killing and cheating and robbing to human nature, and theories that attribute these to frustrations by environment. Pedagogical theories have followed the same sundering: shall we improve the world by making better people, or shall we make better people by improving the world? It seems probable that any man who attempted to do either would find that he had to do both.

But within this welter, this mélange, this interaction that frustrates a dearly prized method of science, some generalizations grow and may perhaps be credited. I think, for example, it is the case that every man will try to do what he wants to do. If he can do it without harm to other men, that's the way he will do it. If he cannot do it without harm to other men, then the result waits upon his willingness or unwillingness to cause harm.

If the result waits, as may be, upon his willingness, then it waits upon his power. But if it waits, as it more usually does, upon an unwillingness, then the circumstances and he himself come under judgment. For the man who is reluctant to cause harm will at once consider the worthiness of his own wish and the worthiness (if there is any) of the obstacles to it. If consideration shows, for example, that the obstacles were placed there out of malice or out of a desire to make a mere instrument of him, then his reluctance may well give way. He will then bring to the contest not aggressiveness alone, nor mere self-love, but the thing we know as righteous anger. He will act not so much because he is "aggressive" as because he confronts powers that are nothing but aggressive, that make claims upon him which they cannot justify and which indeed may be evil to the root.

I I I

THUS THE "LOW" VIEW of human nature, and the "high," seem equally exaggerated. There is in us no *need* to harm others, and hence it cannot be said that we are born corrupt. There is in us, however, no absolute inhibition against harming others, and hence it cannot be said that we are born perfect. As individual persons, then, we inhabit a sort of middle ground, where, in the struggle between needs and inhibitions, we sometimes willingly cause harm to others and sometimes abstain from harm.

The same cannot be said of every social system. Harm will be either injury or deprivation, and these will alike be suffered either in the body or in the character. Now, any society in which one group of people appropriates to itself, without repayment, a portion of the wealth created by others is a society in which many (perhaps most) people suffer varying degrees of deprivation. Such people are harmed in health, in intellect, in general well-being. Yet the social system, since it is the established mode of conducting affairs, pretty much determines what gets done and how it gets done. The members of society, men of good will though they may be, are locked within arrangements for exploitation; and they cannot help doing, at a near or far distance, the harm the system generates. To avoid the harm, they would have to have another system. And so it seems clear that some at least of our evils issue from the social arrangements established by our ancestors, who had in turn received similar evils from ancestors of their own.

There are, however, evils nearer in origin to the person himself—wounds or lesions upon his character. It seems not to be known whether the wound occurs because the environment is strong in harm or the character weak in resistance. It is quite well known, and widely, that parents affect their children's characters for good or ill. Yet splendid people have come out of family life in which meanness and anger prevailed. Other people, of course, have been shattered. Why the one and not the other? An innate toughness in the babe and child?

Whatever the truth of this, something can be done about such wounds, immediately and directly. The victim does not have to wait for society to be changed, as victims of exploitation do. He can get medical treatment and psychotherapy; or, if exploitation limits his access to these, he can get something of the sort from the churches and the public clinics. In the most demoralizing circumstances men can nevertheless be restored, and restoration proceeds apace as men deal actively with those circumstances. What therapy does is to move men out of passivity and into action, or out of compulsive behavior into sensible

action, by removing neurotic impediments to an awareness of the real world.

Whatever happens to society as a whole affects the
individual members, who will as persons be healthy,
wealthy, and wise so far as the system allows. And whatever happens to the members individually affects society
as a whole, which will possess science and art and wisdom so far as it has persons to supply these. Accordingly,
exploitative societies are constantly impoverishing themselves. They do indeed produce many trained and talented
men, but they cannot hope to compete with societies in
which everyone's talent has been trained. The "alienated"
among us, who lament the harm society does them, would
do better, and be less alienated, if they examined also the
harm society does itself.

I V

IF I SEEM to have wandered from the self and self-love,
wandered into the presence of other people and of social
systems, that is because the self is also its relations with
others. If I say that I "have" these relations, I am saying
(what is true enough) that I am distinguishable from
the relations and from the other people in them. Yet also
I "am" these relations. Every touch of another, every
word heard from another, every sight of another's face
or act has been laid down in me as bricks in a building
or as moisture drops in the passing cloud that is I. If it
were not for others, I would not be what I am; if it were
not for those particular others my parents, I would not
be at all. And if I view the case correctly, I do not ask, as
the foolish Cain did: "Am I my brother's keeper?" I *am*
my brother.

I and he have never been separate, except in our
mothers' wombs—and not always there. He and I have

never lived apart, except when we wished to—and not always then. Even dislike has bound us, even hate, for neither of these could exist if we were not together. The harm we sometimes do to one another occurs solely because of a common interrelated presence, which is the ground of virtue and might have made it flower. The lone, stark self is a despairing fiction, bred by circumstances that happen to have caused despair. We may thank the very constitution of our animal and human nature that no such thing can be.

We began (we have said) by needing another breast. Thus we began what is in fact a lifelong dependency upon the labor, skill, patience, and ingenuity of others. Others likewise depend upon our own ingenuity, patience, labor, and skill. Now, dependence assumes support, and support assumes independent activity. If each of us were dependent only, and in no way active, we should all fall flat like stricken leaves. Yet, like the leaves, we have to be stricken before we fall. It is contrary to our nature to be dependent only, just as it is also contrary to our nature to do nothing but act. We need the work of others; we need also to work. In short, we need to be useful to one another.

This need, which we all share and which can so bountifully benefit us all, lies as near the heart of our being as any other need. It is a thing far more "natural" to us than killing or harming or any other of the absurd crimes we commit, always out of frustration. Yet it is exactly this need that the social arrangements we have thus far lived in, exploitative or bureaucratic, have constantly upset.

Suppose that, at the beginning of our history, a sublime genius had deduced from human psychology the social conditions under which such animals ought to live. He knows that we feel a need to be useful to one another, and that consequently we want to be this and will be disappointed if we are not. As a moralist, he knows that our being useful to one another is the very essence of an ideal society. His task is therefore of the simplest: he has only to tell us how to do what we very much want to do. Not only is there no conflict between human nature and ideal society, but the one demands the other. It is, as we say, a cinch.

Well, plainly, it hasn't been a cinch, nor is it. In the late twentieth century A.D., we are nearer to destroying one another than to our heart's desire. No genius presided over our beginning. We had then what we have now: men of superior power, improvising upon facts, on behalf of wishes which they took to be needs. For example, there came a moment when some conqueror discovered, in his dim pragmatic way, that if he kept captives instead of killing them, he could live profitably upon their labor. And when he prolonged this status to the captives' children, he institutionalized slavery. He thus turned a military event into a social system.

All this was improvised. The brawny conqueror was no doubt a man of some intelligence, but he didn't ask what slavery had to do with the psychological fact that we need to be useful to one another. He was rather more impressed with a wish for others to be useful to him. And so when the time came, as it always does, for the thing to be philosophized, Aristotle supplied the justification: some men are slaves by nature.[6]

The worst about this "justification" was that Aristotle knew perfectly well, and indeed said, that the first slaves had been prisoners of war.[7] It was tempting to believe that losers had been predestined to lose; hence

---

[6] *Politics*, 1254a: "He who is by nature not his own but another man's, is by nature a slave." Jowett's translation.
[7] Ibid., 1255a.

the notion of slaves "by nature." Thus one sees how it goes. Instead of moving from a clear insight into human nature toward some reasonable conclusions about social arrangements, the argument has steadily been, throughout ages, from some convenience in existing social arrangements to some imagined attribute of human nature. All such arguments are scandalous and corrupt, and have no purpose other than making rogues prevail.

Pride alone, the valor of self-love, must cause us to reject such descriptions. Since our need to be served by others is matched by our need to be of service to others, there is no psychological ground whatever for inferiority of social status. The people who are much more served than serving are no less deprived, though they are less painfully deprived, than the people who are much more serving than served. Social inferiority, of which it is the essence to be more serving than served, cannot have been *necessitated* by our psychology. It must be something we stumbled into, inattentively, whilst engaged upon other matters. No doubt our psychology permits it and suffers it, as one sometimes permits and suffers a loss.

Thus, as for human nature, human history is rather a mischance; and, as for human history, human nature is a countenance veiled by events. Not a single social system can be explained by reference to human nature alone; rather, every social system has to be explained by a previous social system. Nor has any social system yet allowed free play to our need to serve one another as well as be served. There has, I think, been progress toward this, but we still have much to do.

V

THAT "COUNTENANCE VEILED BY EVENTS." Let us turn back to it once more—the single, lone, striving, hopeful self, which in our discourse we keep slipping away from

into the social milieu. He, she, begins at the breast or
the bottle, lies down all the time and sleeps a good part
of it, coos, babbles, and cries. But so soon as may be, the
little body crawls, walks, runs, talks, and refuses sleep.

Then with what relish this he, this she, gains
acquaintance with the world! Everything is to be looked
at, touched, tasted, listened to, lifted, moved. The world
responds to handling; one can do things with it. There
is a glow of mastery in the child's eyes, as well as from
time to time a tear of defeat. You can do a thing easily
and you try to save a child the trouble, but he says, "I
can do it; let me do it!" He loves to know what the world
is, and he describes it with that candor, adorable and
alarming, which reminds us how much candor we have
lost.

Now, of course, among the thousand things to be
encountered in the world there are other people. These
people are busy with their own encounters; consequently,
encountering them takes on, not seldom, the character of
a collision. The child has no sooner learned his little world
and arranged it than he finds it invaded by personages of
all sorts—by other children and by monsters of adult
size. Happily, their behavior has some regularity of
pattern, and he can learn to expect what they will do. For
a time, however, there must be worry and even fear, until
he has learned the contrary skills of charm and stubbornness. Charm rises from his willingness to serve, and that
from his need to serve. Stubbornness rises from his wish
to be served, and that from his need to be so. He has
begun a lifelong effort at balancing these—a balance as
necessary to his psychological health as it is to social
justice. But he will find this balance often subverted,
and in its stead that mindless equation in which social
injustice matches psychological malaise.

If the child is lucky, most of the people in his world will turn out to be not invaders but friendly presences. He will then possess, at once and securely, some of the greatest values in life. No one who has been loved needs to be told the bliss of being loved, and I suppose that those who haven't been can't be told it. But the bliss of loving is rather less observed. The poets tell us more about its cares and tragedies, as if loving were no great shakes unless it ended as with Dido and Aeneas or Tristan and Iseult. Every first novel is expected to celebrate, and does usually celebrate, the collapse of love between parent and child. Subsequent novels celebrate the hostility that seethes among apparent friends.

No doubt these narratives are true to life. But if so, there is something beneath life's ground that has failed to spring forth and flower. I think, perhaps, that in a relationship of love one is more aware of being loved than of loving. There is always some uncertainty whether the being loved can happen, or, having happened, can last. Thus, when one is loved, one labors at continuing to be so, and attention dwells, readily enough, upon this goal. One gets distracted from a much more interesting and refreshing phenomenon, namely, that one also loves.

The ability to love is, of all our talents, the most joyful in exercise. It is free and freely flowing; and it flows, not as blood from a wound, but as a river from a spring. The element was there, the water; there needed only a loosening of the crust, that the flow might pour out toward limits not yet to be seen. And there is in the flow a circumambient power, gently moving things in its embrace, arranging along its path various harbors and destinations, so that nothing is lost and everything finds a home.

"Had I all this in me?" the lover asks. He had indeed, but with no knowledge of it nor any voluntary mechanism of release. One cannot command oneself to love; one cannot even persuade oneself to love. One can only, so to say, make oneself available.

It is odd that this should be so, for, from the beginning, one rather expected to love. One has seen people doing it; one has even had it done to oneself. Yet the skill to be loving, to release the feeling and let it flow, is not often easily gained. Early attempts are vague like fingerpainting, or gawky like adolescent pranks. And there are always risks—risks, for example, of failure or rejection, risks even of danger and personal-loss. For the act or state of loving has no defenses, is naked and bare. The lover has gone out from his little fortress, the shell he had kept within for protection against wounds. He has assumed an absolute freedom, and, since armament is one of the things he is free from, he is totally exposed.

Such is free love (so unlike the thing usually called this), and indeed the love will not be fully love unless it is free. It comes to us on those fortunate occasions when our love is welcomed and is untouched by any feelings of guilt. We find it in friendship always, in romance often, in parenthood often, in grandparenthood always again. For our friend is he to whom we can speak our inmost thought—or to whom we need not speak it, since he will know it anyway, as we will know his. And when love between man and woman is all that it can be, the raptures of the body have so far mingled with a candor of the mind that, past all thought of having, the lovers are content to *be*.

To love children seems so easy as to be inevitable: they are the beginning of our immortality, and thus, perhaps without our noticing it, they minister to our self-love. They also pain it, when, as they must, they struggle to be themselves. But when they have become themselves and have given us grandchildren, the old, free, limitless love comes back again—the one love that society in no way constrains. Every other love but the grandparental is hedged round with prohibitions: we mustn't love this woman or that man (Romeo mustn't love Juliet, nor Juliet Romeo); we mustn't have a friend of this faith or that persuasion. But our grandchildren may think what they like, and, when we love them, everyone understands.

Consequently, I infer that everyone also understands how love ought to be. The self that goes out in nakedness, without armor or deceit, is in fact the ideal self, the self of all our aspiration, the self of our true self-love, the self we know we ought to be, the self we know society ought to let us be—or, more rationally yet, ought to help us be.

In this regard, however, society gives not much help. The "little competitions, factions, and debates of mankind," as Addison called them, may be little *sub specie aeternitatis,* but they are enough to overwhelm and extinguish our candid loves. We are all of us, like Romeo and Juliet, star-crossed lovers, more or less—Capulets and Montagues by accidental or righteous or imbecile alliance, whom the rages of politics can but destroy. Yet Romeo and Juliet had their love, brief and immortal. We have ours too, amid the rages. By these loves we learn the worth of being human, and by them also we may learn not to fear our "dateless bargain with engrossing death."

PART II

The
Moral
Life

6

Nice Guys
Finish Last

I DON'T KNOW that they do, always. But they do it often
enough to make Mr. Leo Durocher's maxim persuasive
(if the maxim is his, as it is said to be). One can describe
conditions in which the thing will almost certainly happen. Thus we encounter the most painful dilemma,
perhaps, in life: that if we remain morally good, we shall
fail in important enterprises; whilst, if we succeed in
them, we shall have ceased to be morally good.

Power, its nature and use: this is our present theme.
I am speaking of course of social or political power—the
power men have by virtue of being organized into groups.
No doubt a good deal that is merely personal goes into
this: the abilities, skills, intelligence of the individual
men themselves. But when the men are organized, a much
more formidable power appears. There is then a system
of doing things, a disciplined collaboration that magnifies
many times the petty, solitary power of each. Knowledge,
then exchanged, increases rapidly, and with it invention.
Government begins and strengthens itself. Custom and
ideology shape, or try to shape, the younger persons, and
there exists what is thought to be education.

Power is the ability to cause things to happen, to
get things done. Without it, nothing can be caused to
happen, nothing can be got done. In itself, power is
morally quite neutral; it takes moral significance from

the purposes it serves or from the occasions of its use. Perhaps, however, it has a lasting, latent connection with morality in respect of the fact that ethics is sterile unless acted upon.

Apart from this latent connection, power is just the ability to do. This ability is much desired; even ethics, as we see, must desire it. Without it, we can satisfy no need or wish, but are left more passive than infants at the breast, and quite unfed. Possessing power, we can do things; and, the more power we have, the more things we can do. Power protects us against deprivation, and the notion may arise that to be more powerful is to be more secure. There is some truth in this, but also some error, as the fall of potentates has often shown. More power is not necessarily enough power. Perhaps the sole benefit conferred by the fragmentation of mankind is that no one man or parcel of men can have all the power there is.

The possession of power, increasing the range of activity, increases also the area in which the only restraint is self-restraint. Jove can send thunderbolts upon anyone he wishes. The worshipper, therefore, helpless under power, begs Jove to abstain. For the only limitation upon omnipotence will be self-limitation.

Self-limitation, self-restraint, is a virtue certainly, but there is always the fear that it may not exist or may not be exercised. What is feared, rather, is a flash of desire, a swoop of appetite,

> . . . *as when Jove of old*
> *Fell down on Danaë in a shower of gold.*

We now have several Joves made flesh among us, and they can send thunderbolts simultaneously upon us all. They have not done so as yet, presumably because of restraints upon them, among which (dare one hope?) is self-restraint.

It is perhaps the case that people (even rulers) have and use more self-restraint than our fears allow us to suppose. Much of our childhood is given over to learning the nature of it and the occasions of its suitable exercise. We even learn the discipline itself of learning— abstention, that is to say, from things we would otherwise wish to do, in order to get the knowledge and skill we need to have. The schoolboy with his satchel creeps like a snail unwillingly to school, but he arrives.

A great deal of life, in fact, lies in abstention. We "sacrifice" present for future gain, one desire for another, our personal wish for someone else's, life itself (on heroic occasions) for the general good. At the same time, abstention is always more or less painful, because it is the defeat of a wish, and the amount of pain seems to equal the strength of the wish defeated. The very physiology of abstention may be paroxysmal. Yet sometimes, and not seldom, one is able to not do, to hold aloof, to abstain.

The pains of abstention, bitterly felt in one's own personal life, suggest that other people feel similar pains. They do indeed, and often say so (contemporary literature says little else). After the same manner, the awareness of how often one has failed to abstain suggests that other people have failed likewise and may fail again. A vast tract opens up at once to paranoia. One's safety, comfort, pleasure always depend in some degree upon abstention by other people from acts that would harm that pleasure, comfort, safety. It is easy, then, to fear that some of the people who are able to harm will fail to abstain from harming. As Lichty put it in one of his cartoons: "In America a man is free to do what he pleases without considering anyone except his wife, his boss, his neighbors, city, state, and federal authorities."

Despite paranoia, these fears that abstention will not occur have ample ground in fact. For example, what is called "conformity"—that is, agreement in expressed opinion—is maintained among us simply by the fact that most of us have little or no power over our means of livelihood. We can be, and sometimes are, cut off from the means of subsistence for opinions which the actual possessors of power wish not to be expressed. There is no thinker, writer, speaker in the whole world, I dare say, who does not at some time shape his utterance to the demands thus enforced upon him. He ought, of course, to shape his utterance to truth alone, so far as he can know it. But truth, though it is a source of power, has not the power, societies being what they now are, to keep its devotees in life or affluence necessarily and inevitably. If the actual possessors of power loved truth more than power, then no doubt, being among truth's devotees, they would abstain from harm. The world still waits, as it has long waited, for so extraordinary an event.

I I

THERE ARE OTHER WAYS, of course, in which power finds coercive exercise, and the members of our race throughout recorded history have been more aware of power in some few other people than of any power in themselves. The possessors of power have perhaps abstained more often than not from using it coercively, but they cannot, I suppose, become famous for abstention. That would diminish the threat, which depends upon our expecting power to be promptly used. As the threat weakens, the power weakens also.

Self-limitation, self-restraint, though it does exist among the powerful, is therefore a thing not much trusted to. The search for protection against power has, accordingly, followed other paths. One obvious device is to counter power with other power, the expectation being that no one will try to do what he will be prevented from doing. I think there can be no doubt that this does often work successfully. The rulers of nations, I imagine, rise every morning to search out what they can do against countervailing forces. Yet, as we know, balances of power are also balances of enmity. They can pass from a mere negative enforcing of abstention into a death-grapple to destroy the contrary power.

Another mode of limiting power is to separate, on an equal footing, the supreme organs of its exercise. For just this purpose, Montesquieu proposed dividing the chief organs of government according to their functions—executive, legislative, and judicial. If one and the same man, or group of men, enacts laws, enforces them, and judges the cases that come under them, then that man or group has all the power there is. He, or it, has the means of tyranny: he, or it, can be legislator, judge, and excecutioner all in one. There is always reason to fear that what can be will be. But if the three functions of government are assigned each to a separate group of men, the exercise of power will be less arbitrary, and injustices committed by one organ may find rectification in another.

The American system of government is constituted in this style and with these hopes. The executive branch enforces the laws: it can also propose them, but it does not (in theory at least) legislate. The legislative branch enacts laws, but it does not (in theory at least) enforce them. The judicial branch interprets the laws in their application to particular cases, but it does not (in theory at least) enact or enforce them.

"In theory at least"—a saving phrase! For the three functions of government, though separable, are so closely related that it is difficult to perform any one of them without doing a bit of the others. When the Supreme Court declares a law unconstitutional, the law is as null as if it had been defeated in Congress. Similarly, various committees of Congress, in gathering information (as they say) "for legislative purposes," often do the kind of police work ("snooping") that in theory belongs to the executive branch alone.

A third limitation upon power derives from the fact that, politically, power cannot exist without agreement and unity among very many men. What one may call the power of power relates in some proportion to the number of people and to their willingness to follow a common course. Power, to be sure, has its non-human, merely physical instruments —notably weapons. But these require to be used by men, and used for the one common agreed purpose. Leaderships therefore watch carefully over unity; the least dissent alarms them, and the sight of schism sends them into panic fear. For all political power is *organized* power. Any disunity weakens it, and complete disunity will destroy it. The mighty monster scatters itself into grains of sand.

Those grains of sand are ourselves. Strewn, blown, and solitary, they symbolize but feebly the rich identities we would like to be. Such richness they (or we) can have only by being gathered into a commonwealth in which every particle somehow participates in power. The social arrangements for this have not been discovered, and indeed the problem baffles solution. One can see how there can be a society without an economic class of exploiters; one may even think that socialism produces such societies. Nevertheless, two barriers exist between the common citizen and the power he ought democratically to share.

I I I

ONE OF THESE BARRIERS exists because there is, and apparently has to be, government; and the barrier would still remain, if government dwindled into administration. Government and administration alike require an apparatus of functionaries, who conduct society's affairs, and who therefore wield various sorts and degrees of power. Efficiency requires that the tenure of these functionaries be continuous and long; otherwise there will be grindings and even breakdowns in the great machine. In short, it is difficult to see how there can be organized social life without a bureaucracy, and therefore without some impediment to the citizens' sharing of power.

Or, if we begin with the citizens, keeping as the foundation of government their voices and their votes, we shall find it impossibly cumbersome for large populations to settle all questions by voting. Some questions they can thus settle from time to time; as for the rest, there will need to be representatives whom they have elected. Efficiency again, and mere convenience, dictate this. Yet Rousseau was right to think that representation somewhat defeats democracy.[1] The representative is no mere pushbutton; his vote upon legislation may or may not record the wishes of those he represents. Indeed, how can his vote record the wishes, if, as usually happens, the wishes are contrary to one another? Thus the citizens find, with frequent disillusion, that they have given away their power in trying to exercise it. But it is difficult to imagine what other compromise there can be between democracy and efficiency.

Thus the problem of power seems very much like

---

[1] *The Social Contract*, Book II, Chapter I: "The Sovereign, who is no less than a collective being, cannot be represented except by himself: the power may be transmitted but not the will." G. D. H. Cole's translation.

the problem of taming a tiger. You tame and tame, and then, despite all ingenuity, you have a tiger still. He is burning bright, in whatever forests; and you tremble to think or dream what other power dared make him.

When we juxtapose power, the tiger difficult to tame, with the near-anarchy of international relations and the sharp competitions of personal, we come to the heart of our problem. Power, as we see, is not easily counter-balanced. Self-restraint is not as trustable as we could wish. Political devices for the common sharing and ex-ercise of power are not yet known and perhaps cannot exist. Power is in fact exercised to gratify the wishes of men who happen to possess it. We can recognize when these wishes and the means of fulfillment are morally valid, but we cannot be sure that they will always be valid. Quite to the contrary, past history and present ex-perience show that they very often are not.

We must also acknowledge the effect that power has on its possessors. Any power that derives from being socially organized is wielded by men who stand atop vari-ous small or large hierarchies. They are used to getting things done. The things thus got done are the things they desire to be done, either out of their appetites or out of what they honestly believe to be wisdom. They are decision-makers and result-getters: in their own eyes, and others', big, patient, brave, efficient, "practical" men.

It takes self-confidence to wield any power, and great self-confidence to wield great power. Self-confidence is much sustained by success. Since success is likely to follow upon power, power tends to fortify the egos of the powerful and therefore to fortify itself. At the same time, power, though more or less desired by everyone, is par-ticularly desired by ambitious men and sadists: it gratifies exquisitely their yearnings or their lusts. They end, if they did not begin, by loving power for itself.

It was just such phenomena that evoked Lord Acton's celebrated epigram: "Power tends to corrupt, and absolute power corrupts absolutely. Great men are almost always bad."[2] The occasion of this epigram is striking. Mandell Creighton, the Anglican Bishop of London, had just published Volume IV of his *History of the Papacy*, in which he had treated, more gently than fairly, such Renaissance popes as Alexander VI. Now, Acton was a devout Roman Catholic, but a no less devout nineteenth-century liberal. He regarded those corrupt, tyrannical popes with horror, and was eager to call down upon them the damnation that religion promised and they so abundantly deserved. To Creighton's prelatic eye, intent upon successful administration, the iniquities had seemed but formally iniquitous. He could not help admiring how skillful the scoundrels had been. But Acton, rising in fire above these mere felicities of management, generalized wrathfully about the conduct of *all* potentates. Absolute power corrupts absolutely. Great men are almost always bad.

Absolute, absolutely! We will take these words as showing, not facts about power, but the intensity of Acton's ardor. Absolute power would be power without any limitation: there is no such thing. Absolute corruption would signify a human personality without any good trait at all: there is no such thing, though there have been, and are, approximations to it. I think Acton did not intend to say that these impossible things are. He meant to say that power corrupts, that greater power makes greater corruption, and that things can get very bad indeed.

When things get very bad, what is happening? Why, the power is harming people, and great power is either harming more people or harming more seriously the

---

[2] Quoted by Lytton Strachey in his essay on Bishop Creighton in *Biographical Essays* (London: Chatto and Windus; 1948), p. 277.

ones it touches. For all coercion intercepts the satisfaction of a wish: the coerced person is forced to do what he does not want to do, or is forced not to do what he wants to do. No doubt this is often justifiable, and we readily applaud the frustration of would-be thieves, rapists, murderers. But coercion seems less justifiable when it touches policy (where, however, it is always to be found), and is perhaps not justifiable at all when it touches discussion of policy. When it tries to compel behavior that is morally repellent, it has become a positive evil, and, as such, men have sometimes felt obliged to tear it from its roots.

Thus power, coercively used, means pain at the least, and harm, and at the most immoral extremity martyrdom for the righteous. Power is more interested in ends than in means. It chooses means for their efficacy, not for their purity. It proposes to get what it wants to get, no matter what happens along the way. It expects, and readily finds, opposition from other powers similarly directed; and, so far as it is concerned, the sole question is of victory, of dominating or destroying the contrary force.

It happens that in these enterprises a great many things are useful and effective which we would otherwise regard as vice. Lying, spying, slandering, pandering; cruelties of all sorts, brutalities of many sorts. The innocent are cast aside or slain: they are too good for this world. The "weak," among whom are the morally sensitive, fall at the first onset: ambition should be made of sterner stuff. The beautiful burn down to ash in the splendid fires of competition: what were they doing there at all? And the possessors of power, hot and a little winded with its exercise, pause to think how sweet it is to have been strong.

Strong it may have been. But sweet? Organizational lying—by governments, corporations, any public bodies whatever—has become a technology founded (its practitioners hope) upon a science of human nature. Spying also, which is done by many more organizations than governments. Slandering, pandering, likewise. Efficiency is a part of power, and all these vices now run smoothly like great, purring machines.

But the ultimate power of power lies, of course, in causing physical harm. The intended victim, to whom all such acts must be sinister, can either obey power in order to escape it, or let himself be swept aside in death. For that matter, the victim need not be intended. It may be a babe, a child, a woman, an old man, who chances within the target range of power.

For example, our technology has produced a bomb that scatters hundreds of pellets. The shell containing these is called, by a dainty metaphor, the "mother," and this mother, having a kind of womb, discharges from it her lethal children. Human mothers in Vietnam have had their human children stricken thus in their very arms. Western civilization must seem to these human mothers extremely odd. What could they possibly want with it? But they have not yet seen the highest achievement of Western civilization: those man-made suns, the nuclear bursts, which turn men to vapor or to shadows on a wall and leave in the air an odious dust to kill survivors.

I V

WHAT IS A MAN TO DO, seeing that he must live his life and build his character in such an environment? The environment is radically evil. Its pervasive anarchism, often praised as freedom, is in fact servitude. What greater servitude can there be than for a man to be driven or seduced into killing, cheating, despoiling his fellow men? He is a slave, for either he has been allowed no choice, or his power of rational choice has been corrupted by bribes and misinformation. But, more than this, he is a slave to *evil* because of the things he is brought in his bondage to do.

It is part of the evil in the world that these acts are displayed to us as good. Ordinarily one prefers not to kill, cheat, or rob; and lapses from these norms will be attended with feelings of guilt. But if people allow themselves to believe that the victims of such acts are evil men who are themselves engaged in killing, cheating, despoiling, then moral restraints vanish. Evil justifies itself as prevention of evil, and then the beast that prowls beneath every consciousness gets a run in the sunlight and in the open air.

In January of 1967, an American journalist reported from Vietnam that our troops there were "in a pleasant-mannered way, amazingly tough and hard and soldierly":

"If we know where Charlie is, we can zap him easy," said a Marine captain in a company south of Danang. "The problem is finding him. A while back we searched an area for two days, nothing doing, till finally a little kid showed us their hidey-hole 500 meters from where we were camped. They tried to get away through the reeds, and we hit 'em with napalm. We got 38 of the little bastards, by body count, but that was just dumb luck."

The journalist went on to moralize:

A certain casualness about killing is a mark of military professionalism, for killing, after all, is a soldier's business. The professionals whom I knew in the British and French armies in the last war talked in very much the same way, shocking the more innocent Americans. Indeed, the professionalism of the magnificent American army in Vietnam seems to this reporter to mark the end of the long era of American innocence, and the final half-unaware acceptance of the agonizing responsibilities of a great world power.[3]

The end of innocence, the beginning of agony! Can it be that the agony thus beginning had to do with guilt over the loss of innocence? Yet in fact it was neither end nor beginning, for these things have existed with scarcely a pause since the time men learned what can be done with fists. One may sympathetically understand the captain's battle feelings, why he had to think himself superior to the "little bastards" that were slain. But the journalist and his moralizing? There one will see the canker that thrives upon a brain in disconnection from a heart.

When evil tries to justify itself as preventing evil, the alleged evil allegedly to be prevented must be held to be very large. It will seem, or be made to seem, demonic, satanic, mysterious, conspiratorial. Life will be as if you were in Milton's hell—the hell of Book X, where the fallen angels, just rejoicing over Adam's sin, are turned into hissing serpents and lose articulate utterance forever:

> . . . *complicated monsters, head and tail,*
> *Scorpion, and Asp, and Amphisbaena dire,*
> *Cerastes horned, Hydrus, and Ellops drear,*
> *And Dipsas . . .*

This is how you are to feel about rival tribes, races, nations, social systems, and (at a remove) the human persons composing each.

In all this, morality has been turned upside down; I suppose that is why the serpents can no longer speak but

---

[3] *The Saturday Evening Post,* January 14, 1967. The reporter was Mr. Stewart Alsop.

only hiss. The ultimate evils are death and killing, since they destroy life; wounds and disease and poverty, since they harm life; deceit, since it corrupts the deceiver as well as injuring the deceived; anything, indeed, which can prevent or long delay a settled harmony in social life.

At this point we must accept to feel the moral pinch. Our environment, we say, is radically evil, because it is sustained by power—that is, by coercion and violence, by killing, maiming, deceiving. It is radically evil in another way also: it maintains the wealth and power of a few at the cost of poverty, starvation, weakness among multitudes. Of all evils, this is presumably the worst. It cries out to be ended, but it can be ended only by exercise of a power greater than the power that enforces weakness and poverty.

Let us be specific. We have said that the ultimate rule of ethics is to treat every human being as worth doing things for, and hence that no one is to be used as means merely. Who are those most notably used as means merely? Why, those upon whose labor profits are made— the multitudes in Africa, South America, parts of Asia, and indeed throughout that alleged paradise of freedom, the West. Their present status of being "means merely" is enforced upon them by armaments of land, sea, and air, by police, by agents, by propagandists. How can they establish themselves as "ends," as true objects of moral activity, without using some of the same means—the means of power—by which they are now held subject?

If and when they do so (When? They are now doing it), they will be using evil to prevent evil. Let us change the pronoun. When *we* set about ending exploitation, inequality, and oppression of whatever sort, we shall have to use at least some of the means (deceit we cannot use, truth being part of our armament) which oppression, inequality, and exploitation use to maintain themselves.

We shall be using evil to prevent evil. But if we don't do this, we shall be stained with the evil of having failed to prevent evil, of not having made the effort to prevent it.

This is the dilemma with which I began the chapter. We are all caught in it, and we had better be humble. In personal relations there is opportunity for kindness and love, which evoke responses of the same sort. But in social and political affairs, where power rules, these tender virtues lack final effect. There ethics at best will show but a grim face; and in order to be some of the things we ought to be, we shall have to be, for a time, some of the things we ought not to be.

Well, perhaps it's not so bad as all that. When multitudes unite their forces against the greatly powerful few, the very fact that the multitudes are multitudes comes near to applying, immediately and concretely, the Kantian maxim. The multitudes are almost everybody, and when they set about treating themselves as ends, they are doing this for almost everybody. Somewhere deep within these struggles lies the possible unity of mankind—a unity to which the struggles themselves may lead. If so, the paradox of evil preventing evil is a surface phenomenon, a thing not incorrigibly set in history or human nature—a phase, rather, of what Marx called "pre-history," the long desperate ages when men had not yet come out into the light of a rational social order.

Moreover, there have been gains in history—a movement toward this "coming out." We Americans are now in at least one of the stages. We have a Constitution and a Bill of Rights, the first ten amendments. This Bill of Rights establishes ground rules (as one may say) for settling social problems. The cynical and the impatient may regard these rules as a cheat, but in fact the rules have power supported by much tradition and law. Indeed, if they had not power, why would our rulers be at such pains to corrupt them? The rules do in fact limit, as they were intended to do, the behavior of rulers. They do in fact make free, or partly free, expression of our common wish.

I suppose that no one in history has understood the evil of power better than the men who wrote that Bill of Rights. So far as I know, every conceivable type of tyrannical act is defined there with wonderful accuracy and is prohibited. Set as they are amid vast and bitter struggles, these prohibitions may sometime fail—though, I hope, never entirely. Failing or not, partially or totally, they continue to define the mode by which we are to have power over power, thus to escape at last the evil of power, to bend power permanently toward good.

So far as the ground rules are followed and obeyed, there will be prevention of evil without commission of evil. But will the present possessors of power in America obey the rules? Not, one may think, any more than they have to. If, for example, Americans were to vote themselves, by a majority of, say, two hundred million, into common control over their factories and their land, would the present "owners" of these accept the verdict?

If not, then the Constitution would have to be enforced, and the verdict, constitutionally attained, would have to be defended by violence. In short, the Constitution, in order to prevail, must have power exercised on its behalf. This has already happened in our Civil War. It may, and can, happen again, once we all see (as we did with the old slaveowners) who really is against the Constitution.

Yet the fact will then be that a rational means— perhaps *the* rational means—of solving social problems will, in self-defense, accept the dilemma of evil preventing evil. There can be no doubt that it would be right to do so. For if constitutionality yielded at the first onslaught, it would have surrendered, not present good merely, but a promising chance at a rational world.

The inference seems then to be, morally, that one can use evil to prevent evil if, and only if, the good thus attained causes evil to cease. There will be a lot of guess-work about this, but there will also be a clear and unmis-takable test. If, after violence has destroyed the present cause of violence, there follow concord and mercy, then evil has prevented evil, and has at the same time abolished itself.

V

WE TURN BACK, then, to the question we asked: How shall a man live his life and build his character in such an en-vironment? Let us suppose, for the sake of argument, that we are persons of integrity, of principles. We know what the principles are, why they are valid, and how they apply. Let us suppose, further, that one of these known, valid principles is that principles ought to be acted on, that they are worth little unless acted on, and that we ourselves will be worth little unless we act on them.

When we thus act, we act of course in an environ-ment—a family, a circle of friends, a society, a world. The smaller groups are likely to be congenial: there will be love and forbearance in them, and the seeds of morality can flower. But, as we know, the larger environments are shot through with evil; they seem to have more of it, the larger they are. We find, for example, that we cannot earn a living, or have a career, unless we associate our-selves with some organized group that produces or dis-tributes goods or services. These groups are more or less in competition, sometimes sharply so. They therefore have their defenses, among which is the habit of putting a good face on every matter. This sometimes has to be done in violation of truth. It follows that to earn an income is to involve oneself with lies.

One is involved with lies anyway—not necessarily in telling them, but in believing them, in innocently purveying them, in letting them guide conduct. Science of a sort has studied the human eye and ear, the nervous system, the characteristic human responses, the cultural responses of particular groups, in order to devise a technology that shall control what is thought and done. This technology is far subtler than force, and, when effective, renders force unnecessary. It attains a summit of skill when it makes a man think that he has reached the preordained conclusions freely and by the unaided exercise of his own mind.

Now, it can be taken as a maxim that every assertion by a government is to be doubted. With all such assertions the *cui bono?* is answered before it is asked. "To whose advantage?"—plainly, to the government's. No government—indeed, no policy-making body whatever—will describe the facts in such a way as to show that the policy may fail, or describe ethics in such a way as to show that the policy is abominable. Doubtless the policy has been grounded on genuine facts and preferences, through which the rulers are trying to get what they want in the real world. But the public face of the policy is a sculptural triumph in which facts have been molded into harmony with ideals. We are not asked to know what is; we are asked to like what we see.

What shall an honest man do, involved in all these ways with lies? The problem is at first not difficult. He may do pretty well at maintaining an income without actually inventing or telling the usual organizational lies. He may keep himself pretty much undeceived. He may thicken his defenses against the technologists of mendacity, though he can never be sure that some lie has not crept in. He may have learned how to read official statements in such a way as to detect the truth behind the veil—a skill no one would need in a good society.

He is nevertheless caught—caught in the circumstances in which alone anything can be got done. Even if he achieves something socially useful, with the honesty we suppose him to have, he is not likely to produce any important reform without help—that is to say, organized activity with other people. Once this begins, the temptations inherent in all politics make themselves felt. These temptations have an exquisite seductiveness all their own. The man who would not lie or cheat or cause other harm on his own behalf is now invited to do all these things on behalf of an organization with ideals. If he is to effect anything, if he is to bring these ideals a little nearer realization, he has to be interested in consequences, in ends. From an interest in ends it is no long distance to a belief that ends justify means.

Morality itself now subtly collaborates in evil. For one thing, the opponents of reform, of social improvement, are plainly either rogues or fools. If *they* suffer harm, it seems no more than fit reward for their roguery or folly. Moreover the rogues among them, who are surely the more numerous, will, precisely because they are rogues, care nothing about the harm that they themselves inflict; they would avoid inflicting harm only if avoidance were a more efficient means to their ends.

Consequently our paragon, our honest fellow, seeing that the adversary bars no holds, seeing also that he who bars no holds will win over anyone who bars some holds, yields to the conditions of struggle. He is bound to think that, nasty as things may be, there will be at least a triumph for ideals if he himself wins.

Moreover there is loyalty—another point at which morality may prompt evil. Our man owes, or can think he owes, loyalty to the other people who have joined him in the effort at improvement. He owes it also to the organizational structure that binds them all and to the common policy that moves toward the professed ideals. He won't cut loose at the first immorality. He will stay, and wait, and hope. And perhaps before he knows it, the great machine of controversy and strife will have whirled him in its thousand spinnings, until he has left to him no clearer sight of ethics than a dizzied man has of the world.

When this dizziness is well advanced, our man, the onetime paragon, observing the slaughter of babes and children by demolition bombs or by that mother with the thousand pellets, may find himself saying: "Well, these things happen in war." He may go on to think (as I myself did of the affair at Hiroshima) that the results were somehow "deserved." And if the dizziness is nearly absolute, our man will have so satanized his adversaries that he loves their misery more than his own ideals.

Thus, means eating away at ends, we are all corruptible, however sound of soul or noble of wish we were at the beginning. Indeed, the risks of corruption are rather greater for the morally ardent than for their cool or indifferent brethren. For the ardent entertain ideals with passion, and this passion, centered as it is upon ends, stretches but feebly toward the means. The ideals, of course, are general; they appear to gain in nobility as they gain in breadth. The ardor grows with them, and in its glow the fate of individual persons can be strangely dimmed. "I'm bringing brotherhood," thinks the impassioned one; "how can I attend to Tom, Dick, or Harry?" And Tom, Dick, and Harry, who have the ill luck to be particulars and not universals, may soon enough discover what it is like to be means rather than ends.

We repeat our question: If it is difficult to improve

society without causing some harm in the process, what is an honorable man to do? He cannot abandon the effort because of the moral risks, for then his principles would have no effect, and he himself would be a sort of neuter. But if he makes the effort and shows himself willing to do at least some of the things that will ensure success, then he accepts the world's battleground and the filth of combat and the wounds, some of which will be moral. Can he (or we) then fare with some decency?

I think we can. In the first place, we gain from knowing that there are moral risks and what some of those risks are. We gain from understanding the paradox of committing evil to prevent evil. We gain by being obliged, morally, to use every means with scrupulous care, never letting the means be lost in the imagined glory of some end.

From this it will follow, secondly, that we shall want to place some absolute or nearly absolute limits on our conduct. That is to say, we shall want to make plain that there are some things we will never, or hardly ever, do. We'll not kill or maim or lie or despoil—as a rule. Odious phrase, that "as a rule," which in fact means that the thing is not a rule. But one does not have to be a casuist to perceive that there must be exceptions. It is perhaps fortunate that the exceptions will be more convincingly exceptions in proportion as they are few.

In the third place, a certain large area of humane behavior has already been won. Time was (in Renaissance Florence, say) when you had to go armed when you left your house, the house itself having been built as a fortress—battlements, watchtower, and all. You can now live much of your life (some people live all of theirs) without being irresistibly tempted to harm your fellow men. A great many people have never killed or maimed anybody, and they were not persons of weak passions either. We have therefore a broad social ground from which to advance toward the civilizing of all life. What we have yet to learn is that *groups* of men must behave with the same decency that individual persons now show one another. It is of course not known whether groups can learn this; but, equally, it is not known that they cannot.

Lastly, whenever our achieving a social good happens to involve harm to some people, we can try to ensure that the achieved good confers immediate benefits, so that it will plainly appear to have been worth the harm. This is of course very tricky ground, where deceit and illusion have ample play. When, however, the social gain has come out of a struggle to which the mass of the people has dedicated itself, the achieved value will be visible enough, though the losers will not see it.

There remain some difficulties. At the moment of any great social advance, the foes of that advance still have some power and probably will try to recoup their losses. At the same time, the leaders of the advance are likely not to be in agreement as to what exactly has happened or what is to be done next. Disagreement and strife still seethe in the new context and imperil the liberties thought to have been won. These liberties are then put off, and again put off, until they begin to wear the distant aspect of a Second Coming. At this stage, it won't require a cynic to wonder whether social good or just mere transfer of power was what was sought.

Farther than this I cannot, myself, carry the argument, though I know well that it needs advancing. If it were the case that, by long habit, human affairs get settled rationally and peacefully—without deceit and death and all the other modes of mere impatient power—why, then, the problem here discussed would not exist. But it does exist, and is terrible. I don't know that any very great good can be got without some evil, though it is clear enough that evil can be got without any good at all. One may well be discouraged. But one may not, I think, stand silent or abstain.

7

Integrity
and Kindness

---

*I*NTEGRITY AND KINDNESS are, in my view, cardinal virtues, intrinsic goods. To the extent that one has them, one has traits of character that are most to be desired; to the extent that one lacks them, one lacks values that nothing else can supply. For example, the liberating love in which the self goes out, fearless though unprotected, to commune with other selves would be simply impossible. Unkindness and deceit can never do that. They have to hide as much as they can, perhaps for shame, certainly for cautiousness.

Integrity and kindness are by no means powerless in social effect: they can do a good deal, and what they do they do well. Yet they seem thus far unable to accomplish the great purposes of politics. Moreover there are social arrangements that make them extremely difficult to practice. The relation of exploiters to the exploited is itself one of the forms of unkindness, and constantly seeks exemption from the application of principle.

Perhaps, however, there is recompense in the fact that these personal values are, as one may say, always available. One need not wait until the end of a long career to possess them. One can have them here and now and all the time. The difficulty will not be that of a distant goal, but of near and powerful pressures. The kind act and, perhaps more particularly, the principled act quite often involve a loss of other things desired—even, it may be, a loss of life itself. One's hold upon integrity and kindness, therefore, needs strength to be maintained—or, being lost, skill and perseverance to be recovered.

Moreover these two virtues, since they are traits of character, seem to be intimately joined with psychological health. If, as we know, it takes much inward security to accept the risks of loving, that security will be found only in characters little touched with malaise. Respect for others requires self-respect, and love of others requires a self-love untainted by mere self-seeking. Furthermore, the making of choices and decisions—a fairly difficult enterprise much of the time—requires a self-confidence that is easily weakened by doubts of one's own integrity.

And then there is the inescapable fact that one is oneself. One's self (personality, character) is the only companion one cannot avoid, except perhaps by schizophrenia. Choosing, feeling, thinking, it is ever present, and it will be a comfortable or uncomfortable companion according to those choices, feelings, thoughts. What these are must therefore be of much concern. We find ourselves saying such things as, "I couldn't live with myself if I did that," or "I'm not *that* sort of person."

During recent years, a great many young people have shown this concern for integrity and kindness, and have shown it so vividly as to make it a distinguishing mark of their generation. I hope they don't think themselves alone, though they may be tempted to do so. It is not the case that one necessarily loses integrity as one grows older, or that one gives up striving for a better world. The kind and the principled are of no one age but of all ages, and I have observed in my own experience that, when people of various ages work together for a Cause, they are all—regardless of chronology—young.

Nevertheless there probably is some connection between youthfulness of years and purity of intent. The connection, I dare say, grows more intimate as the young people are healthier, brighter, and more skilled than we older folk used to be. Accordingly, I was much struck, some years ago, with what a young girl had to say, speaking at her own commencement exercises at a high school on Long Island: "General Motors wants crewcuts, punctuality, and respectful conformity. Uncle Sam wants patriotic cannon fodder. A world like this deserves contempt. Only goodness in our generation can counter the decadence of the society we are inheriting. And our generation is good."[1]

"Our generation is good"—an adorable faith in one's coevals! I am quite willing to share that faith, though the age is not mine, and though no convincing statistics will, I suppose, ever be available. But perhaps it really is the case that, after the horrors of this century, there has come a generation that is resolved to be just and merciful. If this generalization is at all true, we can expect many more decisions (even in politics) to be founded on integrity and kindness than have been so founded in the past. What then will be their basis? In short, what do the words "integrity" and "kindness" mean?

I I

WE HAD SOMETHING to say of this in Chapter I, where we asserted the intrinsic moral worth of each human being. Everyone, we said, is worth doing things for, and accordingly the guiding maxim is: Treat everyone in just this way. The doctrine is, as we acknowledged, Kantian; and, since large numbers of the youth profess it, they too are

---

[1] *The New York Times*, Sunday, June 30, 1968, Section 4, p. 13.

Kantian whether they know it or not. Kant moves in their present thinking quite as much as Freud or Marx. He has come to them perhaps through the writings of M. Sartre or Professor Marcuse—possibly to the surprise of all three.

In the cool Kantian argument there are moments of insight that one may miss even at a second or third reading. One of these touches us closely here: "In the realm of ends everything has either a PRICE or a DIGNITY. Whatever has a price can be replaced by something else as its equivalent. But what is raised above all price and therefore admits of no equivalent, has a dignity."[2] Thus, if a certain commodity is worth one dollar, it can be exchanged with any other commodity worth one dollar. There will be many such equivalents, all of which can replace one another. But this is decidedly not true of human beings. Their skills, their ability to labor, can be bought and may therefore have a price. They themselves cannot be bought and therefore have no price: the contrary idea was the great illusion of chattel slavery. People have no price; they have dignity—that is to say, intrinsic worth.

The sense of this is rooted deep in quite ordinary language. If a man, as we say, "sells" himself, or "sells out" a friend, the meaning is that he is doing to himself or to his friend something he ought not to attempt. He is treating himself or his friend as if each were a commodity and had a price, whereas (little as he may know it) they both have dignity. And so it becomes clear that to use men as means merely, as other than ends in themselves, is to mistake their true nature and to mistake (usually by exaggeration) one's own.

Now, there are two ways of judging a decision: by the purpose it has in view, and by the manner in which

---

[2] *Grundlegung, Zweiter Abschnitt.* The rendering is Otto Manthey-Zorn's, in his translation of this work (New York: D. Appleton-Century Co.; 1938), p. 53. Kant's emphasis.

the decision is made. If the purpose is consonant with treating people (oneself included) as worth doing things for, then the decision proves itself morally sound. And the habit, the trait of character, of acting in this way can be called "kindness." If I seem to put the case too starkly, let me then add to the habit and the trait a little plain human affection.

The proper mode of making decisions has the same principle as its source. One can (alas, one sometimes does!) decide on no wider ground than that of bare self-interest—or, if the act involves harm to others, of outright selfishness. To decide on such a ground is to ignore the worthiness of others, to regard one's own worthiness as exclusively important, to demand of others what one will not do oneself or to refuse to do what one requires others to do. No rational ethics can be made of this. The heart of ethics is to decide by the one same principle that all other men are required to decide by. There are no exemptions; no one can get off the hook. And the habit, the trait of character, of deciding in this manner is "integrity."

Of failures in these two kinds there are plentiful examples, some of which will no doubt come painfully close to home. Let us, however, take two examples, one from the old past, one from the recent. On April 28, 1861, Mr. Jefferson Davis addressed the Confederate Congress. He had begun presiding over an armed defense of chattel slavery, the *ownership* of some men by other men. Here is part of what he had to say about the owned:

> In the meantime, under the mild and genial climate of the Southern States, and the increasing care for the well-being and comfort of the laboring classes, dictated alike by interest and humanity, the African slaves had augmented in number from about six hundred thousand, at the date of the adoption of the constitutional compact, to upwards of four millions.

In a moral and social condition they had been ele-
vated from brutal savages into docile, intelligent,
and civilized agricultural laborers, and supplied not
only with bodily comforts, but with careful religious
instruction, under the supervision of a superior
race.[3]

The moral claim, especially in the second paragraph, is that slavery was good for the slaves, that they
were being treated as ends, not means merely. This claim,
believable only by those who wanted to believe it, was of
course exactly false, and was grounded in turn upon an
equally false anthropology that denied the existence of
African civilization. Nevertheless it is interesting to observe that the moral principle on which the claim falsely
based itself was the very one we have been asserting.
There is thus a pleasant inference that even scoundrels
recognize morality when they see it, and that in this regard they are often accurate judges. But their arguments,
as here and as generally in politics, are self-serving and
corrupt, and the thing they lack is, precisely, integrity.

From 1861 we pass to 1968, when a letter, which I
now quote, appeared in *The New York Times*. I omit the
date and the name, because I think it merciful not to con-
nect any particular person (though there was one) with
this particular letter:

I for one should like to register my protest against
the outrageous demands of the "organized poor"
who now threaten to invade, occupy and paralyze
the capital in order to compel Congress to grant
their demands.
Their quite unjustified assumption that the wage-

---

[3] This passage will be found in *The Causes of the American
Civil War,* ed. Edwin C. Rozwenc (Boston: D. C. Heath and Co.;
1961), p. 32.

earners of this nation have a moral obligation to aid those who do not earn a good income, or any income, is bad enough. Their demand that the working majority be compelled, through taxation, to provide a living for a minority, on the sole ground that the minority happens to be poor, is to reinstate the principle of involuntary servitude that was abolished a century ago. . . .
I hope that our Senators and Representatives will not legislate under pressure; that they will reject all proposals for a guaranteed annual income—in any form; that they will work toward reducing rather than expanding the present welfare payments to the able-bodied and that they will make no politically advantageous but irresponsible promises to the poor or to any other pressure group.

The writer does not hide the intent of the argument, which is that the privileged are to be protected in their privileges. There is candor here and whatever integrity goes with candor. There are, to be sure, pejorative words and phrases: The Poor People's March On Washington gets described as a "pressure group," and "able-bodied" (not ordinarily pejorative) suggests in this context the old myth that the poor are poor because they are lazy. Moreover there is the ingenious idea that the supplying of competence to the poor imposes "involuntary servitude" on the rich. All such talk is of course tendentious, self-serving, and corrupt.

But what most strikes the moral vision here is the entire indifference to the well-being of large numbers of people. The indifference is indeed so dense as to be quite unashamed. It is unkindness, but of a peculiar sort: it thinks itself so far justified that it takes no thought of concealment. It says the odious thing straight out. Well, at least one knows where one is.

I I I

INTEGRITY AND KINDNESS are a well-mated, well-married pair; in their union they have a common strength against adversity and a common happiness in better times. Separate and alone, however, each moves toward excess and ceases to be itself. Perhaps it is the case that here, as elsewhere, dialectics (the interplay of all things) maintains some sort of balance.

Kindness, alone, becomes sentimentality or an effort at merely pleasing someone else. Integrity, alone, becomes self-righteousness, which is a rather more powerful display of self-importance than one may think. Christian, in *The Pilgrim's Progress,* abandons wife and children in order to reach his own salvation. Why didn't he think equally of theirs?

This question apparently occurred to Bunyan, a quite sound moralist and the best of our writers in prose. Christiana and her children do in their turn also reach the Celestial City (virtue *and* reward), but they do so amid much kindlier events. For, as we are told at the end of Part I, after the husband attained glory, there came a Mr. Ignorance asking to be admitted, who was cast, however, straightway into the pit of hell. Mr. Ignorance—the man who simply didn't know—is one of the most pitiable characters in literature. But when Christiana went in, Mr. Ready-to-halt, Mr. Feeble-mind, and Mr. Despondency followed her. Something (was it the feminine, associated in our culture with the merciful?) disposed Bunyan toward kindness. Part II of *The Pilgrim's Progress* (a sort of lay bible for many years) is altogether more attractive than Part I. Even the writing is better.

These remarks are not an excursus. Months ago, when (as will later be seen) I was painfully impaled upon the question how it is that members of one and the same human species can be so lovable and so hateful, I called upon a friend for help. His response was, "For that, you have to go to the poets." Or, as I think, to literature in general. Accordingly, I may say that, just as I drew from Kant the notions of integrity and of its importance, so I have drawn from Shakespeare the notions of kindness and of *its* importance.

Narrative literature and poetry have an advantage that philosophized morality has not. They can present moral problems in dramatized form, with the values attaching to acts and characters exactly as they do in life. Moreover, poetry usually employs the speech of our unconscious—of our feelings, appetites, and dreams. In that speech, all facts have been suffused with values, and thus it describes things and people as we morally regard them at the given time. When poetry and drama are united, and when both are created by a man who knew all that can be known about men and morals, you have: Shakespeare.

If, now, we try to state Shakespeare's ideas of good and evil, we find we have to do what we do in real life: observe how people make decisions and how they treat one another as a result of those decisions. When, in the plays, the characters do evil things, they usually know that the things are evil—though, as in life, they may or may not feel remorse. Goneril and Regan feel none, but they know each other's corruptness well enough and are not altogether unaware of their own. Lear's sins are more in the nature of calamitous mistakes.

Thus, in the plays, there is no passing-off of evil as mere error, nor any suggestion that evil is a mask for good. Although Hamlet, in one of his silly-intellectual moments, is allowed to say that "there is nothing good or bad, but thinking makes it so," the plays themselves tell us quite the opposite: that good and evil are not mere estimates of the mind, but are persons and powers acting in ways answerable to those terms. Good and evil get entangled with each other and intermixed in one and the same character, just as they do in life. But the distinction between them is not blurred, nor are we left supposing them mere private preferences, detached from standards or ideals.

Moreover there is, throughout, an acceptance of the whole *dramatis personae*—scoundrels, sages, fools— which seems to recommend to us a similar acceptance of mankind. Now, some sorts of acceptance are easy enough: one shrugs one's shoulders, one takes people as they are, wearily, wanly, or with a jest. But this is not Shakespearean acceptance, which is, rather, an interest in every human person, a sympathy so strong that it survives all but the evilest deeds of evil men.

The Shakespearean ethic rests upon an ultimate tension between a sense that evil requires to be wiped away and a sense that its perpetrators, if they prove repentant, deserve to be forgiven. Good, to be sure, may perish in destroying evil; yet, in the end, the moral economy restores itself, and there is no longer something rotten in the state of Denmark. Or, better yet, reconciliation following upon repentance, no tragedy at all occurs, and Prospero finds that "the rarer action is/In virtue than in vengeance."

In our time and culture, the Shakespearean ethic seems all the more convincing because the master himself does not moralize. His characters sometimes do; he does not. Accordingly, events, as they occur in the plays, never seem distorted by a wish to confirm some special maxim of morality. They do, however, suggest a moralized view of mankind. They are, as Dr. Johnson said, "scenes from which a hermit may estimate the transactions of the world, and a confessor predict the progress of the passions."

Conceivably, this is the only proper way to present ethics: "to show virtue her own feature, scorn her own image, and the very age and body of the time his form and pressure." In this mode, if ambiguities occur, they will at least be the ambiguities familiarly encountered in life, not those attending conceptual generalization. We are not sure whether Hamlet will prove morally resolute; he is not sure either. And we never do know for certain what the motive is that keeps him in delay.

These doubts and ambiguities belong to life. They are quite different from those that come with moral theory. When you are considering big concepts—good, evil, right, wrong, values, principles, ideals—you worry whether you have kept the edges sharp and the stretch inclusive. Above all, you worry whether precision has been gained, if it is gained, with loss of relation to life.

For myself, I am no dramatist of any sort, and the best of all possible modes is therefore denied me. I have to follow the moralist's traditional mode, comforted a little by the fact that philosophical generalizations can be useful, however perplexed the theory that contains them. Shakespeare would of course understand this necessity, and, with his usual kindness, would let me be, like Snug the Joiner's Lion, "a very gentle beast, and of a good conscience."

I V

PROFESSOR HARBAGE has said, persuasively, that the trait of character, the quality of act, that Shakespeare most admired is kindness.[4] This trait is of course the one that would have made impossible all tragedy, in the plays and in life. There would have been no blinding of Gloucester,

---

4 Alfred Harbage: *As They Liked It* (New York: Harper Torchbooks; 1961), pp. 175-81.

no maddening of Lear—and, in history, no wars, no persecutions, no crimes. Kindness intercepts evil at its source in human decision; therefore, so far as kindness exists, evil does not exist. If the purpose of ethics is, in part at least, to identify evil and remove it, kindness must be acknowledged a virtue both primary and efficacious.

As we have said, kindness is recognizing the intrinsic worth of other people and treating them therefore as ends. Such language, though accurate, is rather too formal and does not express the affection, love, even yearning, that accompany acts of kindness. For when we are kind to other people, we show a lively, perhaps an intimate, concern for their well-being. We are attentive to their wishes and, beyond these, to certain other things which are good for them but which they may happen not to wish.

But the language is still not simple, rich, familiar enough. Professor Harbage suggests (indeed, it is his main thesis) that audiences at the Globe Theater understood perfectly well the morality of the plays. And he lets us imagine an audience leaving, after a performance of *King Lear:*

> One can see a father and his daughter, their arms touching in the London twilight, ready to trudge let us say to Hackney, or to step in their private barge for the brief voyage to Whitehall Stairs. They know what the play was about. It is a terrible thing, perhaps the most terrible of all things, when a father turns against his own child, or the child against its own father. They knew this before they came to the theatre, Shakespeare knew that they did, and he has left them in firm possession of a truth which life, infinitely more powerful than art as a teacher, has taught them. He has given their homely truth a wonderful, a beautiful investiture.[5]

---

[5] Ibid., pp. 56–7.

Of all the paradoxes in ethics—a subject unusually full of them—this is perhaps the greatest: we seem obliged to theorize about ethics constantly, yet the understanding of it is so general, and the lack of understanding so rare, that possession or lack can be used to determine whether or not a man is fit to stand trial. Probably audiences at the Globe did not understand the plays as well as some later commentators have; probably most people can't give you an ethical theory. But the audiences knew, and people know.

Yet the knowing is perhaps more in the nature of insight, with the gleam of it playing upon this or that problem. There were other people than fathers and daughters in that audience at the Globe. Suppose a statesman— what would he have made of the sufferings of Lear? Would the play have confirmed in him values he already possessed? Possibly, but I think it might also have taught him things he did not know or had not fully realized. The villains of the play he would have recognized straight off: a career in politics would have suggested to him that their behavior was "natural." But our statesman at the Globe might have been too much like King Lear to know in advance what Lear learned through suffering.

Goneril, Regan, and Edmund are people who require that fulfillment shall instantly follow wish: the trait has perhaps been confirmed in them by their being members of a governing elite. At any rate, no law, no principle restrains them, nor does even good sense. They are raw appetite, and for them the intellect is no guide but a mercenary seeker after gain. Thus, quite fittingly in ethics as in fact, they destroy one another.

The King, however, is not like these. He knows the craft of government, and he means well. But long years of being a public figure—the chief public figure, indeed— have denied him self-knowledge. His official self (the commanding monarch) he takes to be his real self. Only when he has been turned out and reduced to the state of a lowly subject does he understand at last what it is to be a man as this world goes. In one storm-swept moment he discovers that there are fellowmen of his who have never known anything but a sweep of storm:

> *Poor naked wretches, whereso'er you are,*
> *That bide the pelting of this pitiless storm,*
> *How shall your houseless heads and unfed sides,*
> *Your loop'd and window'd raggedness defend you*
> *From seasons such as these? O, I have ta'en*
> *Too little care of this! Take physic, pomp:*
> *Expose thyself to feel what wretches feel,*
> *That thou may'st shake the superflux to them,*
> *And show the heavens more just.*

Lear's whole previous notion of government thus dissolves into a true awareness of what government ought to be: "I have ta'en/Too little care of this!" Celebrity, rank, is a sickness one must purge oneself of, as if it were a disease of the bowels. One does so by sharing the lot of common folk, the men of houseless heads and unfed sides, to feel what they feel. Then one learns that the prime duty of government is to administer abundance, the "superflux." So administering, government is at last just. The task is not to be left to supernatural powers; it is men's work, to be done here and now.

It is all so true, so sadly, piercingly true. Would our imagined statesman at the Globe have known it? Possibly. Possibly not. Possibly not even after seeing the play.

And possibly not, after four hundred years.

8

Taking Sides

AT THE END OF BOOK V of *Paradise Lost,* the Seraph
Abdiel quits the assembly of rebellious angels, and passes
through "Heav'n's wide Champaign" to the Mount of God:

Among the faithless, faithful only hee;
Among innumerable false, unmov'd,
Unshak'n, unseduc'd, unterrif'd,
His Loyalty he kept, his Love, his Zeal;
Nor number, nor example with him wrought
To swerve from truth, or change his constant mind
Though single.

Abdiel knew which side he was on—the right one of
course; in struggle or in loyalty, he had the same independence of mind. Satan himself, with that liberality
which Milton often allowed him, perhaps knowing it to be
a trait of rebels, sent Abdiel forth, free to report the delib-
erations. Abdiel was thus no renegade. Indeed, it is not in
the nature of renegades to be unshaken, unseduced, un-
terrified. Quite to the contrary, terror and seducibility are
of their essence. They are the wretches who did not know,
and, on discovering, could not endure, the consequences
of taking sides.

These consequences can be painful and prodigious.
Around them swirl conflicting values, which, because
they conflict, puzzle decision. With the conflict of values
goes a conflict of emotions, and there may also be risks
to oneself and to those one loves. Accordingly, at just the

moment when it is extremely hard to know what to do, the gloom of doubt is further darkened by a storm of feeling. For "sides" in the sense I am giving the term are organized groups of people, groups that jostle one another or struggle with one another in ways that may be enmity. A side can be, for example, a labor union, a political party, a church, a nation-state. You may be on a side because you voluntarily joined it or because you were involuntarily born into it. Whichever the case is, you will feel more than once the pinch of a peculiar dialectic, which is the play of two essential virtues, integrity and loyalty.

Integrity, we have said, is making up one's own mind according to principle; it is speaking and acting in this mode. Loyalty is the habit, consciously sustained, of warm cooperation with other members of the group for attainment of the group's purposes. The group will be strong, and its deeds effective, so long as there is unity —that is to say, common action founded upon common intent.

There is very little in the mere notion of integrity or of loyalty that would make them opposites—nothing more, indeed, than that the one is primarily personal and the other primarily social. The one expresses our selfhood, the other our gift for brotherhood. If we take the two together, we can account for certain basic facts: that no man can truly be himself without belonging to others, nor can belonging truly occur unless it unites *persons*. One can reduce the thing to bare logic. A relation must relate distinct entities. The relation will disappear, if the entities themselves disappear or if they prove unrelatable. Now, belonging is a relation. Consequently, it must unite persons, while at the same time the persons must accept being related.

It seems, then, that each of us personally needs

both the virtues, integrity *and* loyalty. Their undisturbed presence, sustained by society, would be our perfection. There is nothing *intrinsically* good in setting oneself against one's fellows, nor anything *intrinsically* good in the group's prevailing over the person. Ideally, there can be no such contest. Rather, every man's personal decision founded upon principle would agree with similar decisions similarly reached by everyone else. Or, short of that, there would be no disagreement that a little discussion would not cure.

I am, it is plain, describing how things would be if they were as they ought to be. They are in no such state now. They are indeed so far distant from that state, that the twin virtues of loyalty and integrity, both of which we require, are made seeming enemies each of the other. Some of this is due to the structure itself of human organizations (the uneasy relation between leaders and members); most of it, perhaps, is due to contests among organizations and within them. For there are here no monoliths. It is hard enough for a man to maintain unity within himself; harder still for organizations. Differences of view, arising from so simple a thing as limitations of body, mind, experience in each of the members, tend toward divisiveness. Unity requires constant effort in order to be maintained.

All this is magnified when private rapacity adds itself to mere difference of view. Then some, perhaps many, members of the group have to defend themselves against other members. They then have conflict of a sort that discusssion alone will probably not resolve. The worst comes, as it now does among nation-states, when whole groups are aggressive or defensive. Each loses some internal freedom, whilst scrambling for unity. Thus it comes to pass that we are asked or commanded to do

things we know we ought not to do, and forbidden to do
things we know we ought to do.

In the course of this, the concept of loyalty will have
been seized by the heads of organizations and reinter-
preted to mean acceptance of their policies. Dissent will
then be construed as disloyalty. Now, I suppose that occasions of genuine disloyalty are occasions of dissent,
and that therefore *some* occasions of dissent are occasions
of disloyalty. But these are relatively few. Most of the
time, the dissenter is merely saying that he thinks the
policies are mistaken or wrong—that they won't achieve
the goal, or that the goal itself ought not to be pursued.
Indeed, it is probable that he says this out of loyalty to
the organization, as intending to serve its best interests.
And if he is right, he will have proved more effectively
loyal than any of his opponents.

I I

To THESE DIFFICULTIES we must add another, more
nearly philosophical. It isn't just that all men are fallible
and some selfish, or that the exercise of political power
tends to cause harm. The problem to which all this relates
is itself baffling. It is the problem of getting from "here"
to "there," from present circumstances to an end desired.

"All mental life is primarily teleological." This
sentence, if I remember it and its position correctly, is
the first sentence in James's *Psychology: Shorter Course.*
It is also the first sentence I read, years ago, in Sophomore
Philosophy, and the word "teleological," encountered at
eighteen, almost stopped me for good. (I prefer not to use
it, for fear of stopping someone else.) The notion, however, is that most of our thinking, and all of our acting,
is concerned with getting from here to there, from the

state we are presently in to a state we want to be in later.

The transition will occur either by accident or by control—by luck or by planning—or perhaps by a mingling of these. Luck and accident are extremely unreliable, and, if we had nothing but them to go by, we would be less than sparrows feeding on what is found. We have, it appears, more. We have the ability to know events and connections among them, to turn that knowledge into technology, and thus, making things happen as we wish, to get from here to there.

Now, it happens that the here-there relation is of a special sort: it is the relation of present to future, which, read back from the future's view, will then be a relation of present to past. How can relations of this sort be known? What can give us assurance that, by doing certain things in the state we are in, we will reach the state we want to be in?

The odd thing is that we do feel ourselves to have that assurance, although it has ultimately no demonstrable ground. It is vulnerable to Hume's argument.[1] We expect to get from here to there by doing certain things, because, in the past, people have got from similar heres to similar theres by doing those sorts of thing. We assume that the future will resemble the past—sufficiently, at any rate, for our purpose. But if we ask what reason there is to suppose that the future *will* resemble the past, the sole answer is that past futures have steadily resembled past pasts. But this argument assumes what was to have been proved, namely, that futures resemble pasts.

The argument is therefore fallacious.[2] But fallaciousness in an argument does not make the conclusion

---

[1] In, e.g., *An Enquiry Concerning Human Understanding*, Chapter VII.

[2] A fallacy known in the trade as Petitio Principii or Begging the Question.

false. All that has happened is that the reasons turned out not to be reasons. The conclusion may still be true, but we are left not knowing whether it is so. Accordingly, I suppose we are stuck with that about the here-there. We will go on expecting certain results from certain actions, though we are cut off from knowing why. No planner—statesman or private citizen—has ever given up planning, for having read Hume.

One can see why. The human race would have vanished long ago or perhaps never have appeared, if the world were so radically irregular as to make planning impossible. Moreover, in social matters, our ability to predict seems to increase as the entities become larger. One can pretty well predict the future of a society when one knows its structure and instabilities. It is harder to do so with individual persons. Perhaps this is because the person is responding to extremely varied influences, whereas society responds to the totality of those influences. At any rate, Marx never made predictions about anything less than the great sweep; he was shrewdly reticent about details. The result is a view, now sometimes asserted, that Marxism is just great but all the versions are wrong.[3]

I I I

HUME ESTABLISHED DOUBT around the edges of knowledge and action. I think that doubt enters into their very home. One of the ways in which past futures have resembled past pasts is that no one of all those futures has ever *exactly* resembled its own past. "Exactly" means "in every detail." Exact resemblance, resemblance in every detail, would mean that no future happened, because it

---

[3] The same thing happened to the Nicene Creed.

would have remained *identical* with its past. A future, if it is to happen at all, must therefore be in some way different.[4]

So much for reasoning *a priori*. The empirical fact is that every future *has* differed in some manner from its past. Time, taken in general or in the smallest of its sequences, is a series of leaps, and every leap is a leap into novelty. Something new is always coming in. What is new is what has never appeared before. Accordingly, the genuinely new, though its occurrence is guaranteed, so to say, by the resemblance of past futures to past pasts, escapes that resemblance. The past tells you that something new will occur; the past cannot tell you what that new thing specifically is.

Consequently, there appears to be a radical disconnection between knowledge and novelty. Novelty, without which there can be no future and indeed no time, seems by its very nature unpredictable. If that is so, we must expect to encounter what we cannot expect. I don't know what to make of this philosophically, though the paradox does not seem worse than the paradoxes that surround logic.[5] But I think that statesmen are well aware of the paradox. Why else do they have advisers, spies, computers, communications? They want to know "the latest," do they not? And the latest is, precisely, what is new and could not have been predicted.

Although I cannot resolve the basic paradox, which

---

[4] I am using Leibniz's "law of the identity of indiscernibles" —i.e., if two things are in no way different they must be one and the same thing.

[5] E.g., Lewis Carroll's paradox, that every inference rests upon an indefinite number of assumptions, so that no inference is logically complete. Other paradoxes are the "Epimenides," the Russell one about the class of all classes that are not members of themselves (is *it* a member of itself?), and Gödel's theorem.

is (shall one say?) metaphysical, I think I can suggest some of its effects and some means of handling it.

(1) The paradox is one of the roots of discord among men. What cannot be known, or seems not able to be known, somehow excites, just by itself, a dogmatism among contraries. It allows no certainty, but it evokes a sense of certainty. Take, for example, attempts to identify the Mr. W. H. whom Shakespeare or his printer named as "the onlie begetter of these insuing sonnets." In the present state of knowledge, it is quite impossible to know who Mr. W. H. was. Nevertheless, various scholars have, not guessed at, but asserted his identity. Some of them, indeed, have done this by reversing the initials: it wasn't really W. H., they say, but H. W. (which gives them, they think, Henry Wriothesly, Earl of Southampton).

It is most strange how uncertainty, indeed entire absence of knowledge, provokes belief. Perhaps the thing occurs because doubt and ignorance are such painful states to be in—especially for men who are supposed to know, and therefore tend to think that they know. I don't write as one exempt from this lure. The truth is that I have never *felt* so sure of knowing as on those occasions when I did not know and secretly knew that I did not know.

Since, in this manner, doubt (or ignorance) excites the sense of certainty, and since doubt or ignorance supply no ground for belief, the opinions then entertained will be various and conflicting. This fact will only increase ardor in the sense of certainty. Upon this will then be placed all that greed can attempt, and status, and power —every one of which will distort the apprehension of reality, so far as reality might otherwise be known. And so it comes to pass that some of our disputes are about nothing, some about something though not what they are

said to be about, and some—the point is always reached
in the end—about real goals that can be attained or lost
in the real world.

(2) Leaders and members must expect to disagree
a good deal of the time, and not be always alarmed when
they do so. It is the difference between reason and paranoia. Some of the times when leaders and members disagree may indeed be critical, as risking the survival of
the organization. Then a sense of danger and a consequent fear are justified. But if the fear follows upon
early disagreement, the organization, shot through with
paranoia, will misconceive reality and lose controlling
touch upon events.

This sort of condition is more likely to occur among
members than among leaders, who have to be level-
headed, on pain of defeat. But I think that all the Nazis
were addled with it, and governments have now become
so touchy that one may think the Nazi fever has spread.
The fever rises upon a sickness of power—and it is of
course true that we live in an age when somebody may kill
everybody.

Even so, Locke's deep-laid maxims have firmer
ground upon the broader fact:

> We should do well to commiserate our mutual ignor-
> ance, and endeavor to remove it in all the gentle and
> fair ways of information. . . . The necessity of believ-
> ing without knowledge, nay, often upon very slight
> grounds, in this fleeting state of action and blindness
> we are in, should make us more busy and careful to
> inform ourselves than constrain others.[6]

The willingness to doubt, and to let others doubt, is,
we will admit, more difficult for leaders than for followers.
It is hard to imagine a head of state appearing on tele-

---

[6] *Essay on the Human Understanding,* IV, XVI, 4.

vision to say: "The future is uncertain and the choice of
ends is difficult; hence I'm not really sure whether my
proposals can be carried out or whether indeed they ought
to be carried out." You don't rally people in this way.

Thus leaders must profess a certainty they cannot
have. They walk a path between ruin and ruin, between
failing to lead and leading in error or vice. The path can
be trod, of course, but the treading requires genius. That
is why the path is strewn with wreckage of careers,
policies, lives. Ghosts shudder there, and corpses lie un-
buried, and skulls wait to cry *Memento mori!* at later
feasts.

(3) Members of organizations, who are of course
the many, may ponder how wisely to use their greater
gift of doubt. When they use it, the organization does not
immediately begin falling apart. Quite to the contrary,
they may be supplying insights and information that the
leaders do not have. So long as a common trust prevails,
and a common intent, the whole policy will be the wiser
in aim and act. Loyalty will then be unbreached, and there
will be no need to invoke the "higher loyalty" that rises
beyond mere following.

If this were the whole story, ethics would have
been sufficiently served, and my present chapter might
end in grace. But, alas, the truly painful problems have
not yet been touched. Some organizations (nation-states
among them) are arranged for the exploitation of men
by other men, and some of these organizations exploit
other organizations. A basic social rivalry is therefore
laid down in the very nature of things. Leaders then
represent the exploiting classes, and members, who
are mostly the exploited, must offer resistance in order to
save their lives and souls. Some interests they may share
with leaders as being national interests, but the inner
social conflict still goes on.

Beside this, and including it, is the peculiar relation that leaders on their part have, and members on
their part have, toward what is thought or believed,
toward the "ideology" of the organization. This ideology
will have three main parts: (1) an account of the organization's nature and purposes, (2) an account of the historical circumstances the organization is acting in, and
(3) an account of policy and program, i.e., of how to
achieve the purposes in the circumstances. So far as it
is shared, the ideology helps to keep the organization
united. Hence leaders, who, so to say, administer the
ideology along with everything else, are not eager for
changes, or even reinterpretations, of doctrine. Every
such change is a disturbance of unity.

Now, of course, ideologies are human creations,
and all human creations are liable to error. Presumably,
there is no body of doctrine in which every statement is
true. Now, error is disconnection from reality and loss of
possible control over it. There is therefore a duty to correct errors of doctrine, and it will be a loyal act in leaders
or members to remove false statements from the organization's ideology and to replace them with true ones.

But this highly rational and highly loyal effort at
correction collides with the wish, felt keenly by most
leaders and many followers, to keep the organization
united by keeping the ideology as it is. Thus truth, or at
any rate truth-seeking, collides with policy. It has done
so throughout the past, as the glory of martyrs and the
crimes of leaders have shown. There is little to suggest
that it will not continue to do so in the future, no doubt
with further glories and crimes.

In this sort of crisis, morally perhaps the keenest
there can be, a man must yield up truth if he is to follow
the leadership. When he does *that*, he yields up personal
integrity. But also, since the organization needs truth

quite as much as he does, he likewise yields up loyalty when he yields up truth. But if these things are the case, then the opposition between integrity and loyalty must be appearance only and not reality. Their ideal union, which we observed at the beginning, moves throughout human affairs. The twin virtues, whenever they appear, appear together. For loyalty cannot be mere submission, nor integrity mere self-assertiveness.

I V

IT IS therefore not ethics that throws the virtues into opposition, nor does circumstance so far as problems are ethically resolved. But opposition does appear in the way circumstances set the problems. We have seen this to be true of exploitative relations, and true also of the demand for ideological agreement as against the need to correct errors. In all this, the leaders, possessing power, will define loyalty as consent to doctrine or to exploitation. Then the individual person, in order to save his integrity and indeed to save the world, will have to resist. In this way, though I think in no other, the two virtues can be made to seem opposed.

Occasions of this sort have not been rare, and happen oftener when a society—or any other organization —cannot solve its main problems without altering its structure. The structure, of course, is what relates the members. While alteration is going on, the members, the individual persons, will be whirled about in dizzying style. Each of them will have to deal, not alone with the confusion outside himself, but also with the confusion in himself. Some of the problems of taking sides are therefore psychological, and will be worth the study we now attempt.

If the problems relate to an organization you were

born into, why then, you are dealing with the consequences of something you could not help. You may feel gloom about this—or, alternatively, bliss—but you won't feel the ache of ultimate responsibility. You didn't get yourself into the thing; you were got into it. But if the problems relate to an organization you voluntarily joined, then every such problem will sooner or later raise the question whether your joining was wise or indeed made any sense at all.

Such questions may evoke acute self-doubt. What, after all, *was* the motive for joining? What did you really know about the organization you joined? For, without intimate or detailed knowledge, it is quite possible to join an organization because of its professed purposes, demonstrated in at least some of its acts. You join, accordingly, not knowing much of the organization's habits, and, more riskily, not knowing the behavior of *all* human organizations under stress. The thing is more than possible; it is probable. There is often (always?) not time enough to know all that needs to be known.

To begin with, you may not have known the psychological motives that made you join. (I have to use a pronoun, and the pronoun "one" seems cumbersome; but when I say "you," I also mean "I.") A good part of the time, no remarkable deception follows. The grossly appetitive, hearing and fearing the tread of rivals, join piratical parties. Their purpose, and their party's purpose, is to make everyone else walk the plank, so that they may remain as idle as a painted ship upon a painted ocean. There is a naive candor about this, as of lunacy made plain.

The case will be different if you are a man of sense who nevertheless does not yet sense all that can be known about himself. And the true touch comes when you decide to do something about the world's ills. There is now no doubt that the world has ills in a style and degree that far surpasses, though it still includes, older questions as to who is to have what, or whether we are all to have all. The waters we now drink may be fatally poisoned; oxygen may fail from the air we breathe. All this can happen while the nations are "at peace," with no stir of germs or gases, no bursts of nuclear energy.

It is rational to try to prevent this; indeed, not to try would be to surrender the honor as well as the survival of our race. In just this way, though on a lesser scale, some of us thought, thirty-odd years ago, that idle factories and idle men ought to be made busy, in order that everyone might be fed, clothed, housed. To do that, in those days, you had to join a rebellious organization, for the powers-that-were had the opposite idea. You must do the same thing now, just to purify the waters and keep oxygen in the air.

There are thus tremendous reasons for being a rebel. Nothing less can in fact save mankind. But it happens that people may also have private, psychologically secret, reasons for being rebellious. Perhaps they have hated their parents, who, for their part, had hated theirs, and were caught in the trauma. Neuroses latch onto objective circumstances as onto salvation. Moreover, it seems psychologically difficult to hate authority without also loving it. Accordingly, it can happen that a rebel joins a rebellious organization not only because it is rebellious but because it also offers authority.

From this perhaps issues one of the ills, acute but minor, of taking sides: renegacy. Renegades of course leave a side they have been on. When they do this, they often say that they are merely taking another side. In fact, however, the side they newly take will be that of existing power. Otherwise they could not achieve their immediate purpose, which is to desert with as much damage as possible. Driven by anger quite as much as by lust, they drag down, or try to drag down, old friends, old loves, old ideals. It is morally wrong, but, with a rare concurrence of ethics with politics, it is also politically wrong. Renegades have only brief value to their new masters, and are cast aside when that value is gone.

It would be easy to ascribe this behavior to a mere seeking after profit or feeble fame. The most noticeable thing about renegades is that they are angry. My guess is that the true motive, fatal in its consequences, lies in the perilous dialectic of hating authority whilst also loving it. The play of this dialectic drove the future renegade out of allegiance to existing authority. When he carried this hate-love into the rebellious organization, he was (perhaps unknown to himself) quite as willing to hate and oppose the new leadership as to love and follow it.

Suppose, further, that the hate-love turned all along upon his striving to be a person, to be indeed himself. It is a painful state to be in, and in its pain it begets illusions. One of these may be that our man felt himself to be a "natural" leader, unrecognized and denied. For, if one both loves authority and hates it, one can resolve the contradiction by becoming an authority and surrounding that with the love with which one loves oneself. But if our man, set within the new and rebellious organization, finds his authoritativeness denied (as it may well deserve to be), then he will rebel against his chosen fellow rebels.

The most famous of renegades is (at least in our culture) Judas Iscariot, and Dante had him eternally chewed by one of Satan's three mouths in the iciest depths of Hell. The Gospels attribute that renegacy to the lure of thirty pieces of silver. It may have been so. But what if Judas had secretly wished to be the leader, had contemplated bringing in, not the Kingdom of God, but "permanent revolution"? Like many renegades since, he would have begun by disagreeing on a point of theory and ended by helping defeat the movement. Defeat? Well, by no means. For the Leader whom Judas betrayed founded, or is thought to have founded, an organization that still lasts. And there is Judas, overwhelmed by history, chewed, during endless years, in a Satanic mouth.

A crime, a blunder, issuing perhaps from the innocent motive of trying to be oneself—mistaking oneself, however, and one's powers, mistaking anger for insight and disloyalty for truth:

> *Judas took the little, dirty*
> *Bag of pitch and pelf.*
> *Judas counted up to thirty,*
> *Went and hanged himself.*
>
> *Many men who count to thirty*
> *Never feel the blame.*
> *Judas was a lot less dirty*
> *Than others I could name.*

V

WE SAID, some lines back, that renegades desert to *the other* side, not just to *another* side. This follows from a special pattern of relations. One oddity in it is this: when a man becomes aware that his society needs profound alteration, and joins with other men to attempt it, no one calls him a renegade. He has, however, changed sides. He has left the side of present structure and power, and has gone over to a side of new structure and (as he hopes) future power. Why is this not taken to be renegacy? Perhaps because everyone knows that things ought to be better than they are, and that it is really an act of loyalty to try to make things better. Renegades desert to the side that is against improvement, and so end as hostile to mankind.

This analysis suggests that in any epoch there are two main sides: the side that wants no basic change in the social structure and the side that wants basic change. Now, it happens, for reasons obscure to me, that the side that wants basic change tends to proliferate sides within itself. There is hardly ever a single, a one and only, Party of the Left; there are almost always parties on the Left. Think of all those Protestant sects in the sixteenth century and after, each assertedly more "pure," some containing no more than the founder and a few followers.[7] There is such a thing as Leftwing Pluralism. It is history's disease of the infants, a kind of measles.

Why should such nonsense be? Must history mock itself, men mock themselves in making history? A sickened society, it is clear, ought to seek recovery; an economy arranged for private profit ought to reach out toward an economy of abundance shared by all. It is a matter of cure and remedy. The molecules of the social body, the people, are to rearrange themselves in health. There must be a way to do it—more than one way, perhaps, but one best and decisive way.

Doctors disagree, and so do Leftists.[8] These have, or come to have, a "professional" stake in diagnosis and treatment. The need to be right, which is of course there and is fundamental, brings on the wish to be right—or, if doubt proves darkening, the wish to seem right. Quarrels develop over the cure, and the patient sickens while the doctors rage.

---

[7] How these things were in England *circa* 1650 may be read in Lytton Strachey's charming essay, "Muggleton," in *Biographical Essays* (London: Chatto & Windus; 1948), pp. 6–10.

[8] Centrists and Rightists also, of course.

There thus occur moments, perhaps longish intervals, when Leftwing parties denounce one another, and struggle against one another, more than they denounce the bourgeoisie and struggle against it. They are like American fire companies of the early nineteenth century, which were wont to smash one another's apparatus before attending to the fire. The thing is folly, of course, since, if the parties united their powers and united these with the power of the multitudes, they would win in a moment the victory they all say they want to win. Alas, it seems ordinarily to be the case that men, when they become "organized," shrink their sight within the limits of professed doctrine, omit to widen doctrine with their width of sight, and so cannot see what a mere spectator would see—what God sees, if He is looking—the whole wide world.

Thus there come to be sides within a side, and many covers for renegacy. A man may of course move from one of these sides to another without intending to take the historically opposite side. He may leave one of them without taking any other of them, and still not take the opposite side. But if, when he leaves, he deliberately and publicly harms his former associates, then we know that he has chosen, and found gratification in choosing, *the* opposite side.

Well, now, since taking sides yields all these puzzles and evils, let us ask whether there is any way to solve the problem of taking sides. There are, it seems, too many sides, too many organizations demanding faithful following. Their very number obscures choice, and their struggles confound it. Nevertheless, they are part, a large part, of present circumstance. Ethics bids us act in present circumstance. There is no way to act effectively in present circumstance without taking sides. It appears, then, that we must do what it will prove confusing to do, what will involve, more than ordinarily perhaps, the risks of being wrong.

I think we can beat the game. Let us ask, to begin with, what that side would be, if it could be a *side*, to which ethics will commit us with no doubt whatever. There is indeed such a side, the side of mankind as a whole, of mankind as mankind can be—prosperous, creative, one. It happens (so laggard are we) that this side is almost unorganized. The League of Nations was a sip of it; the United Nations is a sort of gargle. But think, now, of the air and the water. Think of all of those military gentlemen, skilled as they are to slay, of all those supposed civilian hierarchs, of the economic hierarchs above the civilian and military—how none of these will last a moment beyond the safety of waters, the breatheability of air. Without this safety and breatheability, the Pentagon itself would vanish, and Wall Street, and Madison Avenue, and Chicago (the last bastion, perhaps, of human tyranny). Where no one can drink or breathe, no one can kill or make money.

Now, *this* side, the side of all mankind, the side that ethics commits us to, happens, as we see, to be unorganized. Accordingly, as to what we ought to do and be, we are almost where the human race began. But if we look attentively at this side, unorganized though it is, we shall know what side to take here and now.

The course of modern history is quite plain. Events of the past five hundred years show, throughout, a defeat of exploitation. The feudal lords, clerical or lay, lost their power. Their successors, prosperous bourgeois and captains of industry, have lost power or are losing it. Every nation that has had empire has lost empire, except the United States, which has begun to lose it. The trend of history is palpable, and can be successfully opposed only by the annihilation of all things human.

It follows that, if anything human is to survive, the trend must be allowed its course toward complete democracy. All these billions of men are to decide, in the end, the nature of their well-being and the means to it. Nothing less can ultimately save us. Accordingly, ethics commits us to the side of the great multitudes—in any given epoch to the side of the "underdogs." These are "the least of these our brethren," the "wretched of the earth." So far as we turn their poverty into wealth, their bondage into freedom, we serve the general good.

Beyond this, there is the universal need for a physical environment we can safely and happily live in and a social environment of just the same sort. This means peace and, since it means peace, means also equality and brotherhood. Ideals they are, and have long been; but they come upon us now as something like an immediate necessity. So much so, indeed, that one marvels that there are any persons willing to act (never mind protestations) to prevent them.

In the effort toward these ideals, there will be various organizations offering to bring them to pass. All of these will be attractive to the extent that they say so and act so. If among them we find one that seems likely to do the thing entirely, we will join it and help it. If, as happens in the frailty of human surmise, the organization seems unlikely to succeed, as being misguided or enfeebled, we may withdraw from it, though not desert. For desertion would signify taking the "opposite" side, the side against mankind.

Time is as Time is, and organizations are as in the swirl of Time they are. What one cannot do, knowing ethics and politics, is to yield up either the necessary effort or the attainable good.

9

Human Nature
and Human Destiny

A CENTURY AGO, John Stuart Mill published a little
book, *The Subjection of Women.* It is scripture (not
yet recognized, I think) for Women's Liberation;
it is scripture indeed for all disadvantaged persons. Its
argument, powerfully produced and universally applicable, proves beyond doubt that it is contrary to reason for
any group within society to be subject to any other group.

The success of Mill's argument, which may owe
something to his happy (and carefully correct) friendship
with Harriet Taylor, allowed him, what his usual prose
did not, sprightly observations. Among them was this:
"One can, to an almost laughable degree, infer what a
man's wife is like, from his opinions about women in
general."

I will take this as a text, enlarging it a little. One
can tell, to an almost laughable degree, what a man's
life is like, from his opinions about people. For, of the
billions of human beings past and present, he has known,
by acquaintance or by report, only a very few. On these
he generalizes, and warmth of generalization will derive
almost entirely from direct acquaintance. If he has lived
among rogues, he will think human nature roguish; if
he has lived among honest folk, he will think human
nature honest and even sublime.

The risk of generalizing upon a few instances is

obvious and vast. Hence, generalizations of this kind are mostly supplied by feeling or by passion—Icarus wings, which try to soar where they cannot. But now suppose that, acknowledging our own sophistication, we attempt something better. We have lived, it may be, among rogues, but have met some honest men; we have lived among honest men, but have encountered some rogues; we have read accounts of past people, and these accounts report both rogues and honest men. A generalization set on this evidence will be more accurate, but will it be accurate enough? Here, at any rate, is the generalization Mill offered, in Part II of *The Subjection of Women:*

> Absolute fiends are as rare as angels, perhaps rarer: ferocious savages, with occasional touches of humanity, are however very frequent: and in the wide interval which separates these from any worthy representatives of the human species, how many are the forms and gradations of animalism and selfishness, often under an outward varnish of civilization and even cultivation, living at peace with the law, maintaining a creditable appearance to all who are not under their power, yet sufficient often to make the lives of all who are so, a torment and a burthen to them!

Now, as it has happened, in a century much more dangerous than Mill's, my own experience of other people, though by no means undisturbed, has been so pleasant that I would guess the number of mere rogues to be less than Mill seems to say, and the number of "absolute fiends" a great deal less than the number of "angels." My generalization is more favorable to mankind and more sanguine about its future, but is it more accurate? I think we don't know and cannot now know. The empirical evidence is thus far inconclusive. And it must be inconclusive, because the central question—the effect of human nature upon human destiny—is a thing we are actually engaged in working out. To prejudge the result would be to tamper with the experiment. A pessimistic view of human nature tends to be self-fulfilling; an optimistic view may breed illusory hopes. It is extremely important for us to say that, as of now, we do not know and are not sure.

The central puzzle is, of course, that rogues, fiends, angels all belong to one and the same species. There must therefore be something they all do, every one of them, but do in contrary ways. I suggest that the one thing they all do is to make decisions, and then to act or try to act accordingly. If they abstain from acting, it is because of a decision to abstain. If they "let things ride," it is because of a decision to let things ride. Non-decision is presumably the life of vegetables. Man is a deciding animal.

On this view, then, decision is the common human trait. The differences, particularly the moral differences, among the members of this species will be found in the style and content of decision. Mill's generalization, and mine, are simply statistical guesses as to what this style and content will be. His guess may well be the shrewder, but it is still a guess.

I I

IT IS POSSIBLE, and may therefore be tempting, to distinguish the human species from other species by attributes that are not strictly moral. For we are an evident species, biologically. No man in his senses would confuse an ant with a man or a man with a mongoose. Vast, fortified divisions of phyla and genera prevent this—though in imagination there may be metaphorical communions, ironic or distasteful. We must observe, however, that in all the uses of this sort—in Aesop, in the *fabliaux*, in La Fontaine, in Swift—there has been some cheapening of ourselves: we aren't as clever as the fox, or as thrifty as the ant, or as noble as the horse. Yet, plainly enough, no fox or ant or horse could be an Aesop, a La Fontaine, a Swift.

Partly this would be due to an entire absence of imagination and of ability to express in symbols what imagination would invent. More strikingly, I think, it would be due to the fact that these other species have not the faculty of conscious decision. They have preferences perhaps, but not principles; they have techniques, but not skills. If, in this respect, they resemble any human beings at all, they resemble the emotivist philosophers, whose doctrine is that we cannot morally judge but only emotionally "evince."

The effort to define, or at any rate describe, human nature gets its strength from our need for fairly accurate prophecy. No man makes his way alone in the world; his personal destiny is always joined with that of others. He can scarcely even conjecture what he himself will be— in success or in failure, in happiness or in gloom—without making at least some guesses about the future of mankind. It therefore remains constantly tempting to argue in this wise: Because human nature is such and such, human destiny will be such and such—as if the causal relation between the two were necessary and absolute.

For myself, I think that no such inference can yield certainty, perhaps not even probability. Whether we take human nature in the abstract or in terms of men living in observable societies, we cannot be sure whether the ultimate issue will be perfection or defeat. What we need, as I shall have occasion to say again in the final chapter, is Keats's "negative capability"—the ability to live and act in the midst of doubt.

It will be useful now, and even amusing, to review the notions of human nature that have appeared, and each for its time prevailed, during the past twenty-five hundred years. With irony and yet propriety, these notions tell us more about the society they were produced in than about human nature as such (though they tell this too). For, exactly as you can tell a man's life by his opinion about human nature, so you can tell a society's conduct by its generalizations about men. Every society sees itself in such concepts as in a mirror: the image has some accuracy because something is in fact there to be reflected. But the distortions are charming, and are even more informative.

In this review, I shall be mentioning philosophers, who are always the magisterial generalizers of the age. They descend to us as having authority ("and not as the scribes"), but we shall do well to consider what that authority is. It is not political authority: it has no physical coercion. It is the authority of having for a long time seemed to be right, and indeed of having in fact been right in some respect all that while. No great philosopher has ever been a dunce or an ignoramus.

At the same time, they were all human beings, with wishes, hopes, pains, and struggles. What they said or wrote rose upon all these, and I think you cannot say you *know* a philosopher unless you know him as you would know a friend—that is to say, as a person. He will probably not have helped you in this (unless he is a Pascal), because he thought that what he had to do was to remove himself as a person in order that the universe might be plain. Happily, however, he could not conceal himself. Across the rampart of *de ordine geometrico* we embrace

Spinoza; across the barrier of mere lecture notes we take Aristotle's hand; we even hear, within the pale, emaciate prose of positivists, the sound of a human voice. Their being wrong means only that they need us; our being right means only that we have needed them.

Well, to begin with—since we have set the starting point at two and a half millennia in the past—there was Aristotle's idea that man is a "rational animal." By this he seems to have meant an animal able to describe the world systematically according to the rules of Aristotelian logic. He thought this (it is one of the surprises of history) in the Athenian twilight—a long, crepuscular decline after the armed triumph of Macedon. It has seldom, perhaps never, happened elsewhere that advanced ideas survived political ruin.

What came immediately after is more characteristic. For how does one adapt to ruin? One may seek refined pleasures, cultivating one's garden, since one cannot help cultivate the commonwealth's. Then one is Epicurean. One can resolve to stand it, however painful the standing; then one is a Stoic. One can reject the whole thing with contempt, preferring (as Diogenes is said to have done) a tub to a house; then one is a Cynic (the etymology is obscure, but it has something to do with dogs).

Out of that social ruin came, thus, three ruined concepts of human nature. Man is a pleasure-seeking animal. Man is a withstanding animal. Man is, if not an existential being, then at any rate an existentialist.

There followed a long age of fifteen hundred years, during which, so far as Western thought goes, the notion of human nature was Saint Paul's. Men are sinful beings, but much too lovable to be damned. If the cosmos is to be thought a moral economy, just and merciful in its effects, men have to be "saved." They have that in their nature which does not deserve absolute ruin, but at the same time they cannot by their own unwisdomed power prevent absolute ruin. Consequently the universe, as a moral economy, has to supply a power not themselves that rescues them. It does so by the sacrificed Son and by that messenger of grace and comfort, the Holy Spirit.

This notion, though profoundly attractive, lost leadership in the seventeenth century, when the world began to be regarded as a system of physical events that could be known and used. According to Descartes, we are primarily thinkers; according to Locke, we are blank tablets, empty cabinets, dark closets, accepting sensations as dents or "objects" or rays of light. The thinker thus becomes one merely "aware," and, with Berkeley, the world itself becomes mere content of consciousness.

In the nineteenth century, when sociology sprang into a science, we find a recovered variety of view. Epicurus, to be sure, appears again in Bentham and Mill: the main motive of men is to get pleasure and avoid pain (though, to do justice, Mill thought a dissatisfied man better than a satisfied pig—perhaps because the man was human after all). But in Comte, in "utopian" socialists such as Owen and Fourier, and in Marx, we have the notion, not comparably proclaimed since the time of Plato's *Republic*, of men as builders of a better world. And indeed they may well build it, whether we think of them as driven by circumstance or as, with some native wisdom, making circumstance useful.

Then came Freud, who lived in a society much more notable for the sickness of its members than for prospects of a better world. Amid all that empirical evidence, he could scarcely fail to think of human nature as a sort of jungle of prowling beasts. The next question would be, Are the beasts tamable? He was never quite sure. One could, he showed, now and then and here and there discipline appetite, but could one do this—could everyone do this—so definitely as to bring men past all harmful deeds whatever? The frail invocation of Eros at the end of *Civilization and Its Discontents* is unconvincing. And so he has left us (we of the West, at any rate) with the gnawing suspicion that human nature may damage or ruin any imaginable social order. This expectation, or conjecture, is regularly trotted out by men so sick with power as to mistake the better world for ruin and ruin for a better world.

Meanwhile, the empiricist tradition, which in its bemused and arrogant way had laid claim to science, went on with shrinkage. It had shrunk mind to consciousness. What next, then? Why, consciousness to physical behavior. Accordingly, there appeared John B. Watson, who had a rebel's skill at self-advertising. He asserted, with some cunning indeed, that thinking goes on in the throat-larynx, and that human life consists in responding to stimuli—that marvelous curve (you could diagram it) $S—R$. But everyone who has had to make a decision knows that, though there is S, a great deal (including mere, bare, plain intelligence) goes on before you reach R. Watson's hope, shared by many a predecessor including Saint Paul, was that powers in the environment would prove saving. In fact, he once dedicated a book to the first mother (as he thought) who would rear a child on Watsonian principles. It seems not to have happened—I think, because the children had their own ideas.

I am reminiscing, as one who has been nudged and left pondering through this century. Journalism is influential, though no one would think it authoritative. Forty years ago, between Christmas and New Year's, when the AAAS—the American Association for the Advancement of Science (advancement?)—was wont to meet, there appeared year after year a certain George H. Crile, who regularly asserted (apparently he thought it comforting) that the "mind" is made of electricity. We weren't unwilling to think this, but we wondered how electricity can do what the mind does. In just the same way, people have wondered for centuries how salvation can do what salvation does. And with as little hearing of an answer.

I I I

EXPLANATIONS by means of economics are, among us, deprecated—probably because they would reveal the true state of affairs. Can it be the case that all the great human hopes of fulfillment, in self and in society, are determined or influenced in any way by the present arrangements for getting food and shelter and clothing? Well, of course. Why do we feel shamed by what we most need? In any event, shame is no ground for rejecting observable influence. Around this the mind and imagination may equally play, the imagination supplying what the mind cautiously rejects.

Accordingly I ask, Why did the seventeenth century's admiration for Man the Thinker collapse into the eighteenth century's idea of Man the Receiver of Sensations? I will wager, as others will probably not be willing to wager, that the reason was, *au fond*, economic.

Three great ideas rose upon the seventeenth century from its origin: (1) that previous descriptions of the universe were probably wrong, (2) that they could be corrected by observation and experiment, and (3) that anyone could make the corrections who had the method of determining truth. All these three assertions were, and are, true. But what were the sociological facts that caused these true assertions to be also believed? Those facts were economic. The more you knew about the world, the more you could control what happened in it. The more you could control what happened in it, the more goods you could produce. The more goods you could produce, the more wealth you could, by trade, accumulate.

"By trade"! What does this entail? There must be a buyer, and therefore one who is willing to receive, who indeed confirms his willingness by offering pay. Accordingly, the man who needed productivity (Man the Thinker) also needed purchasers (Man the Receiver). Keeping still within economic terms, the seller needs not only productivity but the willingness to buy. In theory, he can effect this, and perhaps ought to effect it, by charm of the product alone. But few sellers have trusted to this, and then on few occasions. What the seller has to hope is that the buyer will be receptive, that buyers in the mass will be receptive in the mass.

And there stands Berkeley, saying that men are receivers only. And there stands Hume, saying that only receiving goes on. Indeed, with Hume, the buyer has disappeared as a person, has vanished into occasions of something received. Commercial society cannot ask more of philosophy.

Suppose we put the thing a little more largely. If you were now living in the Middle Ages and were asked about human nature, you would probably, in reply, make some use of the word "soul." In those days, "soul" indicated a quite complex entity, which had intellect, feelings, appetites, and will. It lived and decided within a welter of personal conflict, encountering amid social disturbances other persons similarly disturbed.

It was from this rich concept that the shrinkage began—soul into mind, mind into consciousness, consciousness into behavior. Our Father Adam has got lost in measurements of reaction time, and to find *him* again, we have to go to the psychiatrists.

My old, beloved professor Warner Fite, who wrote more wittily than James and more elegantly than Santayana, used to distinguish between the way people seem to you if you regard them "scientifically" as things observed and the way they seem (indeed, are) if you are aware of yourself as a person. When we take this view as a measure, it will be quite plain that the medievals understood human nature as a man understands himself. Every subsequent view has increasingly regarded people as things observed.

Can one do this, with even partial satisfaction?

In a way, one can. Suppose that I, a man, am in love with a woman, and that consequently I want to live with her, delightedly, in what our not distant ancestors would have called a "carnal union." A thousand things, amounting to one and the same thing, can be said about this—biologically, psychologically, sociologically, philosophically. Yet if I am to *do* any of this, and with mutual delight, I have to have some notion of probabilities. Something I may infer (if I am lucky enough to be accurate) from my notion of human nature, and something may follow from what the lady has led me to think. That is to say, the concept of human nature may suggest that men and women like to bed with each other, and her behavior may suggest that her own wish is much the same.

Thus far, I am moving on grounds of mere strategy; she too, no doubt. Then how do I regard her? As a responder to stimuli? My intent, like any advertiser's, will seem easier to achieve if I suppose this. But she is much more, and therefore more worth loving. As a receiver of sensations? Well, I want her to be that, all right; but my expectation is that she will give sensations as well as get them. As a thinker? I must hope that she is, and therefore knows what she's about.

This is still not enough for explanation. To be sure,

I want the lady to respond; but if she's no more than a doorbell, she's not worth ringing. To be sure, I want her to receive sensations; but if she is merely Berkeleian, she defeats me, and if she and I are merely Humean, we have both disappeared. To be sure, I want her to be a thinker and know me and our common actions; but I also want her to want me, to feel strongly about me, and especially to decide, in the midst of all lures and at the same time independently of them, what she will do.

Love is a mixed achievement of giving and receiving: each person receives for having given, and gives for having received. All that we are is gathered up in this, in the way that all that we are gathers itself before a masterpiece of art. Nevertheless, strange to say, granting our bias toward the new rather than the old, we must in this regard turn the clock back. We must retrace those years—so vast in acquired knowledge, so lean in wisdom —that took us away from the Good Old Soul.

I V

WHEN PEOPLE TALK of progress (which they don't now do as much as once they did), they refer to what has happened since the Middle Ages. What has happened since the Middle Ages is spectacular knowledge about things and an elaborate technology for dealing with things. Men now walk on the moon, but men continue to kill other men. Indeed, they can kill men more easily— for the matter of that, more men more easily than they can walk on the moon. Efficiency, it appears, is not necessarily moral advance.

Human advance (if that is what it is) is therefore so awkward and stumbling that no one need any longer feel defensive about liking old things and old ways. There are things about the Middle Ages that one cannot regret:

the commitment of large numbers, for example, to violence or passivity, the talent lost in an irrational social
order. Yet there are things we have lost since, by having
lost the medieval view, that I could well wish we had
retained: the sweet commentary upon immediate life
that hides beneath the seats of choir stalls, clings to the
capitals of columns, winks within windows of glorious
glass, lives in the illuminations of manuscripts. Such
things tell me, not only how people were, but what I now
am.

Moreover, it would not have occurred to a medieval
artist to suppose that art can be served by saying nothing.
Nor would it have occurred to him to think that he needed
to leave *his* name behind him. The men who made the
glass at Chartres are not now known by name or by
biography. Their intent was, it would appear, not that
the maker should be known but that the masterpiece
should *be*.

This result, heroically modest, happened, one may
think, not alone because the medievals understood human
nature, but because they had a certain view of the cosmos.
This view, we must now grant, was inaccurate, but it
was powerful. It held that the universe is a moral economy, that is to say, an order such that all men get their
just deserts—the righteous theirs, the wicked theirs. This
concept the medievals have left, in eloquent sculpture,
above the portals of many a church.

One may go to Bourges, for example, where the
cathedral of Saint Stephen tops the hill, the town cluster-
ing around the base. Saint Stephen was the first Christian
martyr and the youngest: he defied, and in legend defeated, the wiseacres of the synagogue. He was Youth and
the insight of Youth, set against organized decay. And
there he is at Bourges, on the right of the façade, being

stoned and at the same time granted the crown of martyrdom.

All this is convincing enough, for the young can
correct our errors: it is their historical task. But at
Bourges, the designers and sculptors put Saint Stephen
himself to one side. What they displayed above the central
portal was the ultimate decision, the Last Judgment,
the *Dies Irae*. Accordingly, on the lowest architectural
level, graves are breaking open, and the dead rise. On the
next level, they are separated into saved and damned,
the Archangel Michael presiding, with a famous smile,   .
over all. Among the damned are a king and a bishop. The
medievals knew that status is not saving, and that some
at least of the highest are among the worst.

Thus medieval men regarded the universe as a
moral system in which no righteous life is finally lost, nor
any evil life saved. This, it may seem, is how things
ought to be—though one may doubt whether anyone, however wicked, deserves to be permanently damned. But the
mournful discovery of all the centuries since is that the
cosmos is not a moral system. No intent lay behind its
creation and development. It does not particularly sustain
righteousness or reject villainy. And now in the late twentieth century, amid our struggles, we have begun to doubt
whether the human part of the cosmos can even improve
its present state.

We can, however, take the concept of improvement
as a useful part of the medieval legacy. To say that a
thing is, is of course to say that it can be: existence
proves possibility. Thus, when the medievals said that
the cosmos is a moral system, they were saying, by im-
plication, that some of it, at any rate, can be so. It is
possible, let us still believe, for us to make a safer,
happier world by knowledge, integrity, kindness. Indeed,

this notion was an article of faith (or, as they would have said, an inference from science) among social thinkers a hundred years ago. It still lingers, scarred by more recent failures and crimes. Let us see if it can still yield hope.

V

THE MEMBERS of the human species have certain characteristics that members of other species have not. Rational thought—that is, the knowledge of what sentences can be inferred from other sentences and what cannot—distinguishes us from all the other beings we know (it may not, of course, from other species we do not yet know). Also (with the same limitation), the ability to make tools as well as use them. Also, the ability to laugh.

These traits set us apart, but they seem not to state the essence of being human. Laughter comes closest: it is an awareness of the contrariety in things, and is therefore a form of knowledge. What is peculiarly human about human beings is, I think, the fact that they are able to make up their own minds. The verb that states their quintessence is the verb "to decide." When they do this, they do it with conscious intent; and when they do it morally, they do it according to principle. Unconscious motive may be an influence, even a powerful influence, upon decision, but it cannot be decision itself. At the same time, not every conscious intent is obedient to principles, and hence not every conscious intent is morally valid.

Such lapses, however, do not harm the definition I propose. I am not saying that men are so constituted as always to decide by moral principles. On that view, men would do no evil, and books on ethics would be merely descriptive. Nor am I saying that everyone physiologically human is capable of making decisions, whether by principles or not. Some, it appears, are genetically incapable; some have been crippled by environment, with much the same result. Some are neurotic or psychotic, and, with them, reason totters on her throne or is toppled from it. Such persons are, in their various ways, failures in humanity. There is a thing they cannot do, which, if they could do it, would leave them fully human—namely, make up their minds by reason and by principle.

Thus men are those beings who are capable of morality, who may develop the virtues and attain the good life. Now, I don't suppose that any man has always and infallibly acted on right principles. But probably everyone has tried to do so at one time or another, and most (so I would think) have succeeded oftener than not. The constant failures we would expect to find among the exploiting classes or their *lumpen*-victims; the very class relations cause them to fail. Even so, the *capacity* for ethics was there all the while, and was the human thing about them.

We have said that decision occurs within a private welter of appetites, feelings, ideas, and within a large social welter of all those private welters. Deciding can thus be pretty difficult at times. It is as if the hero of the drama were constantly beset by beasts large and small, of varying strengths—beasts he must tame, or throw off, or defeat, in order to do what he knows he ought to do.

The "beasts" are part of human nature too, and the "social welter" is the work of past and present men. Beasts and welter are powerful. One is beset by possibly compulsive drives from within and by steady pressures from without. There may be joinings of the two, the power being multiplied. The temptation then arises to explain human behavior in terms of psychology (the inward man) or in terms of social forces (the outer environment). There is some cogency in such explanations, since both sorts of causes do operate all the time. But if the explanations fail to make central our ability to decide, or omit the fact altogether, the effect will be to describe men as helpless. Overwhelmed by determinism, we would be unable to decide as against our appetites or as against social pressures. There would then be no virtue or vice, no moral responsibility. One can see the result in men's very excuses: "I couldn't help it; I'm only human" or "I couldn't help it; look at the fix I'm in."

Such explanations are incomplete, and have left out an active element. Making up one's own mind is as much a psychological fact as any other psychological fact; that is to say, *self*-determination can and does occur. Socially, men change their environment by acting upon it. The psychological fact and the social fact unite to produce a third fact, namely, that men, by making up their own minds, can change the world according to their intentions—although, paradoxically, in the interaction of all those billions of wills, what results is not exactly what anyone intended.

Hence, though much wrought upon, we are not slaves of appetite or feeling; nor are we slaves to the social order, though the rulers of it may like us to be. We can, and indeed do, discipline what is irrational within us; we can, and indeed sometimes do, remove what harms and defeats us in the world around. I suppose that one way to describe the various social movements that have from time to time improved the human lot would be this: individual persons made up their own minds, joined with others who had made up *theirs,* shared with them the relevant knowledge of fact and value, and went on, in unity, to success.

V I

THAT DECISION is central in human nature may be judged from evidence closer to us still, and touchingly empirical. What do people seek, when they give themselves to psychotherapy for the easing of certain aches and pains? I don't think I would be alone in having hoped that the "cure" would free one from the effort at making up one's mind, that right decisions would thereafter be nearly automatic—as if one had become Aristotle's virtuous man, who is so by habit.

It turns out, however, that nothing of the kind is the case. Therapy will (or may) reveal hidden motives, buried injuries, and a certain cast of temperament. One knows oneself better, can detect the play of inward powers upon decision—thus to avoid neurotic obstacles. But after all this—the months of interview, the thousands of words —it is still the man himself who has to do the deciding. He and he alone can avoid the obstacles, fend off the passions, interpret the motives toward something rational.

Technology is an extension of our powers, and in part a replacement of them. But, despite all fears (and the fears are themselves significant), technology can never replace *us*. It offers various means of controlling the world—that is, of making the course of events do what we want it to do—but the one effort it cannot free us from, without at the same time ending our existence as human persons, is the effort at decision. In a certain sense, everything can be committed to machines, even choices and preferences. There would, however, always remain the power that had put all that into machines; and, if we think of machines as having done the putting, we are in an indefinite regress, which can be stopped, at whatever distance, only by human decision.

And, anyway, who wants to surrender himself to

machines? Certainly not our rulers. They have, to be sure, computerized *our* responses; they play electrified games with various "enemies." But would they submit their own decisions to automation? Only, I think, in lesser ways. Strategy and tactics they might thus surrender (the more fools they!), but they would never thus surrender their last and final appetites, which blazon forth in blood their indomitable wish to rule. We can make the thing embarrassingly personal: If *you* were a ruler, what would you do? You would submit to machines the means of ruling, but would you submit to machines the *moral* question whether you ought to rule? And, after all, what would a machine know about morality? Indeed, what does a machine *know* at all?

We can now bring the thing home to each of us, an elector who has no choice. We—you and I—whose established political activity is set in the casting of votes have, in our voting, preferred this or that person to others. We have, as the emotivists say, "evinced." But would any one of us give over our power of moral decision to anyone we have thus "elected"? Or to someone somebody else has happened to elect? To do this would be to surrender to the old slave-owners of the American South or to the later (and now historically outmoded) wage slave-owners of the American North. I'm lumbering here under history. I can put the question far more simply: Would you let a congressman tell you what to do?

Of course you wouldn't. When you thus refuse, not only as with congressmen (the least of these our brethren) but with any public official whatever, you are asserting your mere, simple, and unsubvertible humanity. Nobody, you say, is to make you a non-man. You may be wrong in this or that decision, but no one is to take from you, with your own consent, the right and power of decision itself.

Is our human life other than this? And if it were, would it any longer be human?

V I I

IF ONE LOOKS at all that human beings have done during these long millennia, one sees, at once and quite plainly, the effects of interaction. All those folk collided or (for it did happen) lived in a sort of harmony. When they collided, their hostility was plain enough. When they lived in harmony, their hostility was a good deal less plain. Thus, over all, they loved and hated, and the prevalence of the one over the other owed a great deal to the social arrangements they had brought about. There was perhaps never a time when, except for precommitted felons, anyone would have preferred a social arrangement of hate to a social arrangement of love.

There is thus an enormous amount of evidence that can be called empirical. If we generalize upon it, we are left—in the air. How we are so, and in what degree we are so, constitutes the puzzle about our prospects, about human destiny.

I have been lost in this quandary for many a year, and, during these, I have encountered various views. The one I find most convincing up to now, though I hope it will not prove to be accurate, is that of the wisest of English moralists, Samuel Johnson. He was a man by whom one could decide what one is. If it had happened that one hated one's parents, one would not like Sam, the Great Cham. If it had happened that one's own rebelliousness did not prevent learning, one would know that this authoritative person, who only wanted to be right and therefore had to think he was right, was indeed right about a good many things.

I now offer what, in his words, we ought to think

about; and I offer it, as hoping it can be improved upon. I will first record what may be called his "metaphysical" position, and then the social consequences that he drew:

> The reigning philosophy [i.e., science] informs us, that the vast bodies which constitute the universe, are regulated in their progress through the ethereal spaces, by the perpetual agency of contrary forces; by one of which they are restrained from deserting their orbits, and losing themselves in the immensity of heaven; and are held off by the other from rushing together, and clustering round their center with everlasting cohesion.[1]

Thus Johnson knew about the interplay of opposites, in the very age and at its height when the opposite of dialectics ("mechanism") has seemed to prevail. This general view about the nature of things allowed him to infer something about the nature of people:

> The same contrariety of impulse may be perhaps discovered in the motions of men: we are formed for society, not 'for combination; we are equally unqualified to live in close connection with our fellow-beings, and in total separation from them; we are attracted towards each other by general sympathy, but kept back from contact by private interests.

"We are formed for society, not for combination." This notion Johnson formed in the early years of commercial supremacy. There is nothing feudal about it, no suggestion of ranks established by birth. What it says is that people, acting on their own, though obviously needing one another, cannot work together enough, or work together long enough, to effect a lasting social

---

[1] *Adventurer*, No. 45 (1753).

harmony. All "combinations" (he says elsewhere in the essay) tend to fall into fragments, shattered from within.

This somewhat pessimistic description is, I think, a fair summary of the effect of human nature upon human destiny up to Johnson's time and up to our own in the West. But must it always hold? If we are formed for society, may not this predisposition give us the means of making ourselves at last faithfully and harmoniously one?

It seems clear that we shall be much happier if we do this. Whether it will be done depends on all those multitudinous decisions of morally free men. The question waits to be decided. We shall not know unless we try. Accordingly, let us try.

10

Joy

Father goes to bed and goes to sleep. My brother goes to do his homework. And here you are, staring into the stars.

IT IS PLEASANT to begin a chapter with the material of a footnote. The little passage I have set at the head is taken from a short prose piece called "Darkness," by a fifteen-year-old writer known to us solely as J.S. The piece is one of many by youngsters in the New York ghetto—Blacks and Puerto Ricans. A sensitive and discerning teacher, Mr. Stanley M. Joseph, collected and published them under the title *The Me Nobody Knows*.[1] From all this came, not long after and with the same title, a successful rock musical, the sets for which (if I may say so) were designed by my son Clarke.

I had, however, chosen the passage from the book alone, with no knowledge that there was to be a play. I chose it because of its beauty and its origin. Taking beauty and origin together, one sees how much talent lies around us half-buried under poverty, and one can guess the vast gains there would be for our culture if poverty were abolished and all these young people treated as ends, not means. Training they would need, no doubt, refinement of skill. But, as for singing, the voice is already there.

---

[1] (New York: Discus Books; 1969). "Darkness" will be found on p. 92.

So also is the technique, in something more than rudiments. Consider that little passage again. It has, for one thing, the blessing of monosyllables. There are no words of more than two syllables, and of two-syllable words there are only four. The style is thus spare and easy. The first two sentences are simply informative about fact: father goes to bed; brother goes to do his homework. Then abruptly, like a rocket burst, comes poetry graced with alliteration: "And here you are, staring into the stars." Presumably, J.S. did not know, as a rhetorical device, that a poetic sentence will seem more poetic if it follows two plain ones. He felt the thing, though, as candor and innocence feel.

Now, contrast this writing with official prose—the language of men of status or of importance at least imagined. Every such man finds it quite impossible to say, "I hope that . . ."; he says, "I am hopeful that . . ." He never has a conversation; he has a "dialogue." And when he has a dialogue, he talks, not about the mess we're in, but about "the human condition." Speech of this sort is an acquired infirmity, like stammering in a frightened child.

J.S. is poor; he ought not to be poor; he knows beauty and can beautifully record it. A fact, a moral estimate of the fact, a judgment of taste—these three things gather around him, gather indeed around us all. Conceptually rendered, they are the true, the good, and the beautiful. By long tradition, these are the ultimate philosophical notions, and one may wish to complete the survey of ethics by trying at least to sketch their unity. Even a sketch, however, will be a mingling of sense and thought, desire and fulfillment; and from it may issue a state of being, rich and discernibly prolonged, that can answer to the word "joy."

We have heard, and do still hear, enough lamentation. The world is full of peril; and governments, of folly. But gloom is a response that does nothing for us. It slows, if it does not paralyze, activity. Hanging the head is no posture for saving the world. Hence gloom is, on the whole, encouraged by those who rule us.

Or suppose it turns out in the end that the world is not saved? Shall we have moved about it meanwhile with the same bowed heads and moist eyes and beaten breasts and cringing carriage? I think that if we were to do this, we would disgrace our species. Joy in the prospect of life and victory would of course be vast; but, short of that or even thinking it unlikely; there can still be joy. After all, each of us expects his own personal death; we have nevertheless had moments of joy within that limitation. And these were moments when we were at the height of our powers, in harmony with circumstance and with our fellow men.

For gloom we can go to the existentialists or to our daily paper. Where do we go for joy? The answer has a great deal to do with that remarkable youth of fifteen years, J.S.

I I

THE THINGS WE DO as human beings are of three kinds: we know, we judge, and we enjoy. When we know, we are aware of what is in fact the case. When we judge morally, we are aware what choice is free of bias and considers all people as worth doing things for. When we enjoy with discernment, we are aware of something that engages sense and thought and feeling, that stretches these toward their limits, yet keeps them in harmony with one another and with the world.

In knowledge, we ask, Is the statement true? The

answer then is, The statement is true if, and only if, what it asserts to be the case actually *is* the case.

In ethics, we ask, Is the decision right? The answer is, The decision is right if, and only if, it respects the intrinsic worth of all human beings.

In esthetics, we ask, Is the thing beautiful? The answer is, The thing is beautiful if, and only if, it engages and excites our powers into lively, yet harmonious, play with one another and with the world.

Well, now: to know is to be aware of what is the case, and to be aware of what is the case is to have at least one ground of harmony with the world. Not to have it is to be disconnected from the world and cut off from controlling it. There can be no successful ethics without knowledge. Hence the true is important to the good.

To judge morally is to be aware of human worth and dignity. This awareness is also an appreciation of human powers—the marvels men can devise by knowing, can effect by choosing, can enjoy by having perfected. Thus the good, to which the true was already necessary, gives itself and the true over to the beautiful, which is the enjoyment of all.

Let us try the thing another way. In order to *know*, we have to prefer true statements to false ones; true statements will be our preferred objects of belief. There is a moral commitment in this preference. Hence discovery of the true depends upon acceptance of the good.

In the effort at discovery, moreover, we shall employ all our powers—some of them not strictly logical, but intuitive and imaginative. The great scientific generalizations were first touched upon in the same way as the great conceptions of art. They were enjoyed before they were known. Hence, apprehension of the true has much the same ground as appreciation of the beautiful.

Thus there is unity among the three concepts, but it is of course a unity among differences. Knowing, choosing, and enjoying are three different activities, each with a different standard of accomplishment. The standard of any one of them cannot validly replace the standard of any other. Not all that exists is good or beautiful; not all that is good or beautiful exists. The good and the beautiful do, however, seem rather close, for both of them deal with values and necessarily have respect for human powers. I think it will be found extremely difficult to regard as beautiful anything that is morally repellent—gas chambers and crematoria, for example.

Concepts, though meant to be revealing, are often cloaks. Let us lift them for the moment, and watch our talented youth, J.S., as he stares into the stars. There is knowledge in what he is doing, though presumably not of a developed, scientific sort. Nevertheless he knows what he is looking at. There is probably moral admiration of the kind that Kant expressed in his famous phrase about "the starry heavens above me," perhaps also the sweet, mixed sense of human littleness and greatness that Pascal celebrated. But the experience was, of course, mainly and supremely esthetic. Beauty was what J.S. was most aware of, though knowledge and ethics were present too. Indeed, in that moment of staring into the stars, the true and the good lay together within the embrace of the beautiful. Their harmony in turn expressed the moment's harmony between J.S. and his world.

For him it was a prelude to joy, as we may now see by reading the entire piece called "Darkness":

> The sun goes down and the moon comes up. And children go inside. Friday night party begins. You go in and eat dinner. We sit down and talk about the things that have happened. Mother goes to the kitchen.

Father goes to bed and goes to sleep. My brother
goes to do his homework. And here you are, staring
into the stars. It looks like the moon is a toy and the
stars are little children playing on a blanket of black
coals. And then the children go away, father and
mother gets up and it's the sun. A new day is born.
No more darkness.
Light sings all over the world.

The remarkable metaphor in which the stars become children playing on a blanket of black coals seems
entirely original and unexpected: it is the true voice of
J.S. The final metaphor, however, "Light sings all over
the world," is contrived, is J.S. consciously reaching for
an effect. It is the sort of lapse one finds, here and there,
in Keats—whom J.S. resembles in other and more excellent ways. But where is the writer who has said nothing
that was not original?

To me at any rate, it seems clear that poetry has
come to J.S. in the way that Keats said it should: "as
naturally as the leaves to a tree."[2] And though the metaphor "Light sings" somewhat fails, the human experience
behind it does not.

I I I

JOY IS A STATE OF FEELING measurably long, though of
course not permanent—something between a flash and
an eternity. One might arrange a scale for it, from delight to rapture. I don't know that this would be an up-
ward scale. Delight suggests calm, rapture intensity. It
would be hard to say that either of these is more "joyful"
than the other.

Of all entities in the world, feelings are perhaps

---

[2] Letter to John Taylor, February 27 [1818?].

the most derivative. They seem, as it were, to come over us from some other source. The human sense of this is recorded in the very etymology of such words as "emotion" (a "being moved"—formed from a Latin passive participle) and "passion" (an "undergoing"—formed from a deponent verb). No doubt the nervous system is quite active on these occasions. Nevertheless, in appearance at any rate, the feelings take their nature and intensity from things other than themselves—from the body that has them, from things outside that body and acting upon it, and perhaps from a long history of such interactions.

There is a paradox here. Our awareness of our feelings is direct, intimate, entirely private and personal. No one else has *my* feelings; and if, for example, I had never felt love, I would have some difficulty knowing what it is. Yet, when I come to say what love is, I have to refer to all the things from which it derives. The private collapses into the public, the personal into the social. Presumably this is why we can be aware of other people's feelings, though we do not have, and cannot have, those particular feelings. Imagination and sensitivity do the thing for us.

As a state of feeling, then, joy is privately possessed but publicly and socially explainable. We can recognize it partly by identifying what it is not. It is intensely pleasant, but the pleasure of it is in no way diseased. For example, there is nothing sadistic or masochistic about it, and from this fact we may guess that it involves some sort of harmony with other people and within ourselves. Moreover, the pleasure is not trivial or wayward; rather, it declares itself connected with great and valuable things. It is esthetic, to be sure, perhaps peculiarly so; but it has an encompassing moral tone.

The source of all this lies, I think, in what the

feelings do in our behavior. They report, so to say, the effect of other things and people upon us, but they are not scientific determinants of truth. They move, and even swarm, around decision, but, simply by themselves, they are not able to tell us what is right. They offer hints, suggestions, and even flashes of wisdom. The thing they are not, is normative. They are companions, not guides. They cannot rationally command, but at the same time they are not to be commanded: no one can either love or hate because he has been told to do so, or tells himself to do so. It is the nature of companionship not to command, to take no orders, and yet to be respected.

What do the feelings report, as they accompany us? Well, in general, they report how we are faring in the world. If circumstances are such as to permit or invite the exercise of our powers (our skills of intellect and decision), the feeling will be so pleasant as to participate in joy. If circumstances are such as to permit or invite us into harmony, friendship, love with other persons, the feeling will then be, unmistakably, joy.

For consider the corresponding negatives. Hostility is, on the whole, a baleful feeling. It threatens harm to other people, and it constricts the powers of the man himself. It is useful, no doubt, in overthrowing tyranny; but, if it continues after that success, it will scar the better world it has helped to produce.

And what of the hostility that has its origin in discontent with oneself? This came into existence because the man (who is perhaps every man) had trouble deciding things in the way he should. There were the attendant feelings of guilt, ending, perhaps, in despair and rage over the difficulty of doing anything right. Why was the right so difficult? "Objective" circumstances made it hard to do; "subjective" circumstances (which were also "objective," being the training he had had imposed upon him) made it hard to choose. He has, it may be, some sense of his own worth and his worthiness to survive, but he thinks that death will put an end to his worth even as it does to his survival.

This is a man as existentialists conceive "Man" to be. He is angry, and he feels guilt about feeling angry. But he cannot feel joy. Indeed, he cannot even laugh. He may be aware of the absurd—or at any rate say that he is so—but, since he cannot laugh at it and then, by laughter, set about amending it, we can infer that his awareness is, after all, quite dim.

Joy, therefore, has no negative feelings. It will have in it love and not hate, kindness and not anger, mercy and not vengeance. It will be the record and report that he who feels it is in harmony with some at least of his fellow men and is at peace with himself. It seems, therefore, that the social and personal conditions which make joy possible are the same as those which satisfy the guiding principle of ethics. That is to say, so far as joy is really joy, the possessors of it are treating other people and themselves as worth doing things for. Treating people in this way is exactly what the word "brotherhood" means. Such a notion was Schiller's, when he wrote the words that moved Beethoven to splendid musical utterance: "Alle Menschen werden Brüder/Wo dein sanfter Flügel weilt"—all men become brothers wherever joy's wings touch down.

Joy is thus, potentially at least, a massive feeling set on a massive base. That base is formed of many people, ultimately of all mankind. Personally and privately, it seeks and holds the pure in heart, the masters of their own motives—or, since we are all fairly frail, those that are pure now and then or (if there be good fortune) often. For nature has not been so stingy as to deny us joy until we have become perfect. The occurrence of joy whenever we have briefly but effectively ennobled ourselves foreshows, I think, what perfection would feel like if it were to come.

I V

IT APPEARS TO BE the case that every part of life lies, or can lie, under discipline. If you want to *know* anything, there is only one way to do that: you must learn the method of knowing, accept to use it, and use it. If you want to decide rightly and act rightly, there is only one way to do *that*: you must learn the method of right choices, accept to use it, and use it.

Now, the feelings too can be disciplined, but in a rather different way. They are radically rebellious, almost intractable, and they cannot be made by fiat to be other than in the circumstances they are. At the same time, however, feelings are wonderfully open to lure and seduction, and may thus be brought under discipline. Such discipline is very likely to be conferred by the arts.

There is a tendency in science, ethics, politics, to manage the feelings by fending them off. If you want to know what is the case, you must not let feeling distort or obscure your apprehension. If you want to act rightly— to treat everyone as worth doing things for—you must not let hostile feelings influence decision. And in politics, leaders must try to be men of cool calculation, though they are often willing enough for passion to move among the masses, the led.

But even in these enterprises, "fending off" is not all that happens, nor is it the best. Around knowledge and decision, when these most successfully occur, there is a climate of interest and satisfaction, within which the contrary feelings are stilled. Knowing and deciding are, both of them, native human talents. They can be enjoyed for their own sakes as well as for the benefits they confer.

It is, however, esthetic appreciation—the discerning enjoyment of works of art—that gives the feelings their most usual and effective discipline. Subtlety of response ("refinement," shall one say?) increases as we mature and can thus compare a hundred past responses with other hundreds. There are works we discover to be fine which at first we did not recognize to be so, and there are works we first found extremely pleasing which, after longer and richer experience, please us less. There are *juvenilia* of taste as well as of creation. The late Beethoven quartets will seem rather too formidable at first hearing, but, heard often enough, they will seem as easy and welcoming as those of Opus 18.

Now, the "longer and richer experience" I have referred to includes everything in our personal lives. It means that we know more about all sorts of things, that we have become acquainted with many values, and indeed that we have formed some fairly coherent notion of the world and of our place in it. It means that not only have we become philosophers but have been behaving as philosophers all along.

It may be that this view, which is mine, is rather too markedly so. Esthetic experience is extremely varied and extremely personal; other people would probably not generalize upon it in the way I have. Yet, for myself, I have never been able to think that esthetic appreciation can be limited to form and structure, essential though these are. Life is not so readily sundered into parts. What is to prevent form and structure from guiding our thoughts toward a great many other things that seem to serve as "content" to the structure and form? Does one not meditate on subjects more than musical when one listens, say, to the A-Minor among those late quartets?[3] And is the experience not richer and wiser on that account?

This notion of course records the history of my own enjoyments in the arts and the taste that has developed upon these. Nevertheless, when it comes to limiting the range of appreciation to some one portion of the work— to the technique, say—I wonder whether the thing is psychologically possible. By what act of attention does one separate the element alleged to be the sole esthetic element from all the other things the work suggests? Earlier in this century, Clive Bell asserted that "significant form" was the only proper concern of taste in painting. It is difficult, however, not to think that the adjective "significant" brings back all or most of the things the stern noun "form" was meant to exclude.

Now, Bell belonged to the Bloomsbury Group, among whom, as we have said, were disciples of George Edward Moore. Bell's doctrine of significant form corresponds rather well with Moore's theory of the indefinability of "good": important matters have disappeared from consideration, and the first stage of contemporary alienation has begun. And there is a gruesome correspondence also between what has subsequently happened in the arts and what has happened in ethical theory. The arts and ethical theory began by not doing what (so to say) they were meant to do, or at any rate had the opportunity to do, and they have ended by attacking themselves. Thus we now have the anti-novel, the blank or nearly blank canvas, and *la musique concrête*.

Ethics and the arts, in anger at the world, have recoiled angrily upon themselves. I would conjecture that a

---

[3] Beethoven himself thought so, at any rate, seeing that he designated one of the movements as a song of thanksgiving upon recovery from an illness.

future historian (if there is indeed a human future and therefore a future man who writes history), looking back upon these bare blank rooms, these bare blank canvases, these writhing images, these intended defeats of human skill (whatever else they are said to be), will have no trouble recognizing that the men of our time lived amid universal discontent.

The ancient Egyptian sculptors, and those of Phidias' time and the time just before him, distorted the human form toward dignity and even majesty. Our contemporaries distort it toward shapes of triviality and contempt. Why so? Well, if we consider all the slaughter, all the thievery and lies, that in our century have been visited by men upon other men, we shall not be surprised that artists portray the human form as agonized or contemptible—a mingling of slayer and slain. I don't know that in any previous age so many works, unpersuasive of their own beauty, have been accompanied with so strong a demand to be liked, on pain of the observer's being charged with lack of taste.

Yet it is a response, however pretentious, to calamity, and as such may be sympathetically understood. This, however, is not the way in which Beethoven responded to his deafness, nor Milton to his blindness. We know that they both felt angry, but what happened thereafter to their art was quite a different thing. With each of them, the art so far fulfilled itself as almost to surpass itself. It was the opposite of destruction.

Well, perhaps these were simply men who managed to conquer personal tragedy. It is doubtless vastly more difficult for a single creator to handle the tragedy of the world: he may, reasonably enough, feel overwhelmed and even helpless. But in fact he is not alone. There are millions of people in the world who are his fellows—some of them creative like himself, and all of them more or less talented. The question is not whether *he* can deal with the tragedy of the world but whether *we* can. I seem to remember Marx's saying, somewhere, that history never sets insoluble problems. There is splendid comfort in the notion, but now there must be much doubt.

We shall not know unless we try. It will take patient, sustained effort by all of us, sharing our insights and information, sharing our courage, and setting (so far as we can) despondency aside. The arts have a role to play in this, which will benefit them as arts while at the same time it assists the rescue of men. For the arts cannot help recording, even when they say they don't, what it feels like to be a human person in a given context of space and time. They can also record—and in the past have sometimes recorded—what it will feel like to be a human person in a context much safer and happier than any we now know. Moreover, between the practice of any art and the practice of morality there are resemblances well worth examining.

V

THE ACT AND PROCESS of esthetic creation are a little drama (perhaps, rather, a great drama) setting forth the problem of treating other people as ends while also treating oneself as an end. The creator must say what he wants to say and work as he wants to work; otherwise he is not an end but is only a means, perhaps a mercenary one. At the same time, if he asks to be approved, without making his work accessible to the observer (granting that he may require some effort on the observer's part), then he is treating other people as means and not as ends in themselves.

There will follow, if the work has merit, an interplay in which the creator's taste allows, elicits, and informs the observer's taste. The creator is likely to know the medium much better than the observer—its past achievements and present possibilities. He therefore can offer the observer what anyone more knowledgeable in some regard can offer anyone less knowledgeable, that is to say, enlightenment. But enlightenment will not occur unless the enlightener does in fact give forth light. This he will not be likely to do unless he accepts the observer as the observer is, with such capacity for being enlightened as he may happen to have. The observer's own powers are called into exercise. To this extent, and in this manner, he is being used as means, but as means toward something he shall himself become, and therefore as an end.

Enlightenment of whatever sort—scientific, moral, esthetic—seems to fail the moment the man to be enlightened is treated as means only. Then we get training and not education, obedience and not morality, rhetoric and not art. For men thus produced can perform certain tasks but not understand the world, can follow orders but not make up their own minds, can feel responsively but not discern the beautiful. If, however, they had been treated as ends, they would have been brought to understand the world in some measure, to make up their own minds (rightly, if possible, but at any rate independently), and to accept as beautiful only such works as had beauty as their main intent.

This last point is touchy. There is a view, quite arguable, that if a work of art comments upon life and the world, or if it passes beyond comment into advocacy (into urging some sort of conduct upon us), then the work has put itself out of esthetics altogether. Whatever we call it, we cannot call it beautiful, any more than we can call an advertisement for a toothpaste beautiful. There is a sense, rather paranoid indeed, that on such occasions we are being had: instead of being offered beauty, we are being got to do something or to accept some interested view of what is the case.

For example, various organizations (political or not) have at their meetings what is called a "literature table," on which are displayed tracts and pamphlets that advocate the organization's doctrines. It is odd, and I think charming, that the word "literature" still has common use in this peculiar sense. The tracts and pamphlets are indeed lettered, but no one expects that they will be literature. Nevertheless, a good many tracts and pamphlets have been literature in the esthetic sense also, and literature as an art would be impoverished by exclusion of them.[4]

A theory of esthetics that would remove from our literature any of Milton's prose or Swift's is hopelessly unconvincing. The inference then must be that no work of art is *necessarily* harmed, made barren of beauty, when it urges upon us either a course of action or a point of view. Esthetically, the question turns upon priorities. The proposed course of action or the proposed point of view may contribute to the beauty of the work, but it is the quality of the writing and of the whole conception that makes the work beautiful, if it is so at all. The things asserted may be ever so true, and the conduct advocated may be ever so right, but beauty depends upon the use of the medium and its materials.

Thus, if you use the medium aright, you have what esthetically you want. The rest may come after. When Blake, in a famous passage, having invoked the bow of burning gold and the arrows of desire, tells us to build Jerusalem, the instant response is to go right on out and

---

[4] One may consult the charming *Miscellany of Tracts and Pamphlets* in the World's Classics Series (Oxford: the University Press; 1927). The editor was Mr. A. C. Ward, and the twenty selected authors include some of the most eminent in our literature.

do it. Every reader of the poem feels that he can, and feels this so strongly as hardly to perceive that he is also being told he ought. Blake had the priorities rightly arranged. It is not so much that building Jerusalem is a fine idea, and, being expressed in the poem, helps to make the poem beautiful; it is that the poem, being already beautiful as a poem, makes you want to build Jerusalem. Beauty first; then let what follows, follow.

It was once upon a time thought that works of art "ought" to present human nature in a favorable or ideal light. This notion probably cannot be defended baldly, but it did express the moral lift that successful esthetic experience usually gives. Almost everyone I have talked with who has seen the stage version of *The Me Nobody Knows* has said that it made him "feel better"—that is to say, feel morally improved, with a livelier faith in human nature. When Handel was told that people had enjoyed the "Hallelujah Chorus," his reply is said to have been, "But I wanted to make them better." Haydn, we are told, wore his best clothes when composing, as proper dress for meeting God. And I have heard of a professor at Haverford College, many years ago, who always wore evening dress when he sat down to write: it signified a moral respect for the medium.

These charming and perhaps apocryphal stories show a sense, very generally shared, that beauty is not only an esthetic value but a moral value too. Beauty does something that's good for you, and I think we ought now to pass beyond the old post-Victorian fear that what's good for you does something bad for art. This fear seems still to be powerful. Our contemporaries, assuming that they don't obliterate things altogether, evidently prefer what is, or seems, factual. This preference reproduces the three-hundred-year-old sundering of ethics from science, of value from fact.

Things being as they are, it will no doubt be difficult for the arts, overwhelmed by tragic fact, to begin re-
asserting the ideal—as Blake always did, who knew the
facts well enough. The difficult thing, however, is just
what genius regularly tries and does. We have more than
a few geniuses in our world, and talented folk in abundance. You cannot count, even by computer, the ones who
are not yet thirty, and there are many who are thirty or
more. It will surprise me if there does not develop a recovered interest in human dignity and, beyond that, in
the possibility of joy. To be sure, this cannot happen until
the possibility and the interest begin to be felt once more.
We cannot command the feeling to exist, but we can open
our hearts, and wait.

V I

IF OUR DISCUSSION has been correct, there are certain
identifiable relations between beauty and goodness. Let
us see whether we can find any between beauty and truth.
The task is the more tempting because of Keats's famous,
puzzling utterance, which, like the Urn of which it was
the message, "doth tease us out of thought/As doth eternity." That is to say, I suppose, that we're not going to
make much of it, although we shall continue to suspect
that much is there.

On the wall of Keats's bedroom, in Hampstead,
hangs, emblazoned, a part of a sentence he wrote to Ben-
jamin Bailey in 1817: "I am certain of nothing but of the
holiness of the heart's affections and the truth of Imagination—What the imagination seizes as Beauty must be
truth— . . ." It is an eloquent passage; one feels one would
be convinced, if one could discover what is being said.
And what is being said is presumably what the more famous utterance says: "Beauty is truth, truth beauty."

The rest of that sentence in the letter to Bailey is not quite grammatical and is therefore confused; but, two sentences later, comes the remark, "The Imagination may be compared to Adam's dream—he awoke and found it truth." What Adam found was Eve, and she was worth finding—never mind her slightly and unjustly damaged reputation. Keats seems to be saying that beauties imagined before they occur do sometimes occur nevertheless.

Their occurrence, however, is what is decisively important. Once they are there and are "seized" by the imagination, they have a reality more startling and more powerful than that of other facts. They are, so to say, true; and, of all true things, they are the truest. Like the Urn itself, they exist, with their import, through time and almost outside it. Keats is quite right about this, for, merely as a matter of logic, it is the case that if a sentence is true at all, it is always true. "Forever wilt thou love, and she be fair!"

Keats is perhaps the most endearing of our poets for his sensitivity and his hard-won skill at expressing it. (Poetry decidedly did not come to him as naturally as the leaves to a tree.) This achievement has somewhat obscured his skill as a philosopher—until recent times, at any rate. When he is considering the joys of life, his generalizations about them tend to be richly vague; but when he is considering life's woes, which indeed swarmed massively upon him, his generalizations are sharp, exact, and wise. His notion of "negative capability," for example, is one of the most useful we can have, if we wish to think that philosophy has to do with the conduct of life. As he defined it, negative capability exists "when a man is capable of being in uncertainties, mysteries, doubts, without any irritable reaching after fact and reason."[5]

---

[5] Quoted in Graham Hough: *The Romantic Poets* (New York: W. W. Norton & Co., Inc.; 1964), p. 170.

The ability to live with doubt! One needs this particularly in the moral life, where the remoter consequences of action cannot be known, and even the immediate effect is somewhat uncertain. One needs it in the contemporary world, where the whole possibility of morals —that is to say, the continued existence of mankind—is threatened. For myself, I think that "reaching after fact and reason," though it might be irritable, would be necessary; but fact and reason have their limits too, beyond which doubt must reign again.

Doubt gives rise to contrary feelings, which range from hope to despair, according as problems seem able or not able to be solved. The feelings, in turn, become moods—settled and pervasive emotional states, which may help or hinder decision. The negative states are no help at all, but tend either toward passivity or toward mere angry response. As Robert Bridges put the case in 1904:

> *Incertainty that once gave scope to dream*
> *Of laughing enterprise and glory untold,*
> *Is now a blackness that no stars redeem,*
> *A wall of terror in a night of cold.*

The sonnet ("Melancholia") from which these lines come ends rather lamely. The reader (or perhaps it is the poet himself) is told that he has wanted too much and despaired too soon, that other people are quite aware of joy, and that if he is not so aware he must be dull indeed. But a failure to feel joy cannot be the fault of any one person, if indeed it is a fault at all. The fault, so far as it touches him, will lie, not in failing to feel, but in failing to act.

Negative capability is the power to decide amid doubt, in the lack of many things one does not know but knows would be important if one knew them. Negative capability is thus the courage of the intellect. It does not ask assurance of success, for it is aware that there is no such assurance. It does not ask an absolute certainty of being right, for it is aware that there is no such certainty and, further, that many who have thought they had it were dangerously misled. It knows that "in the very temple of Delight/Veil'd Melancholy has her sovran shrine"; but it knows the temple quite as well as the shrine. In just the same way, J.S., who knew the ghetto, also knew the stars.

If our world, a vast welter of events, instead of being the world it is, were a pleasant tide moving surely toward a pleasant harbor, joy would need no commentary but would be a feeling obvious and universally possessed. We seem to sail upon no such tide. But suppose that, in some later years, the tide turns out to have been more like this than we think. What then?

Why, then the great conflicts we listed in our first chapter would be resolved, or nearly so. The struggle among nations would have ended in a world society, the struggle among social classes in abundance for all, the struggle of men against their governments in a disappearance of government as such. No wars then, and no coercion; rather, the skilled private judgment of every man freely fulfilling itself in the dignity of all. The thing seems a mere dream; yet it is possible. It seems fatally distant; yet the means of it are at hand.

It is dismaying, no doubt—this chance of losing it all when we could have it all. Yet I don't really know why the fear of losing it all should so outweigh the hope of having it all. There would be joy in the attainment; there can be joy even in the struggle. There are already the joys we have in friendship, love, and the beauties of art. There are nights, to be sure, darkling enough. Yet here we are, staring into the stars.

Index

A Note on the Author

BARROWS DUNHAM, now visiting professor at the School of Social Research at the University of Pennsylvania, was chairman of the philosophy department at Temple University from 1942 to 1953. In his books, Professor Dunham has distinguished himself not only by the ease and elegance with which he makes abstruse philosophic concepts available to general readers but by his ability to relate seemingly remote theory to the everyday life of those readers. *Man Against Myth*, hailed by such varied critics as Albert Einstein, Dorothy Parker, John Dewey, J. D. Bernal, and Donald Ogden Stewart, was published in 1947. *Giant in Chains* followed in 1953, and *Heroes and Heretics* in 1964. Professor Dunham was born in New Jersey and received his A.B., A.M., and Ph.D. degrees from Princeton University. He is married to an artist, the former Alice Clarke; they live in Cynwyd near Philadelphia.

A Note on the Type

THIS BOOK was set on the Linotype in a face called Primer, designed by Rudolph Ruzicka, who was earlier responsible for the design of Fairfield and Fairfield Medium, Linotype faces whose virtues have for some time now been accorded wide recognition.

The complete range of sizes of Primer was first made available in 1954, although the pilot size of 12-point was ready as early as 1951. The design of the face makes general reference to Linotype Century—long a serviceable type, totally lacking in manner or frills of any kind—but brilliantly corrects its characterless quality.

In the designs for Primer, Mr. Ruzicka has once again exemplified the truth of a statement made about him by the late W. A. Dwiggins: "His outstanding quality, as artist and person, is *sanity*. Complete esthetic equipment, all managed by good, sound judgment about ways and means, aims and purposes, utilities and 'functions'—and all this level-headed balance-mechanism added to the lively mental state that makes an artist an artist. Fortunate equipment in a disordered world . . ."

The book was composed, printed and bound by
The Haddon Craftsmen, Inc., Scranton, Pa.
Typography and binding design by Constance T. Doyle.